Disclaimer

The material in this book is presented for informational purposes only and not intended for the treatment or diagnosis of any disease. Please consult with a qualified health professional for any ailment discussed or mentioned herein. The author and publisher take no responsibility for the use or misuse of any information presented in this work.

Timeless Voyager Press

10 NATURAL TREATMENTS YOU HAVEN'T
HEARD OF UNTIL NOW

Entire Contents © 2000 by Timeless Voyager Press

ISBN 1-892264-05-6

TIMELESS VOYAGER PRESS
PO Box 6678
Santa Barbara, CA 93160

Cover by Bruce Stephen Holms
Digital Photographs & Editing by Bruce Stephen Holms

10 NATURAL TREATMENTS YOU HAVEN'T HEARD OF UNTIL NOW

Ten Conditions With Proven Treatment Plans

William Wong, N.D., Ph.D.

Formatted and Edited by
Bruce Stephen Holms

Table Of Contents

Timeless Voyager Press

Acknowledgments

This work is dedicated to my tutor in Naturopathy the late Dr. Charles W. Turner N.D., D.C., D.O., Doctor of Chinese Medicine, D.Sc., inductee member of the Hall of Science in Duseldorf; soldier, healer, pioneer and giant among men. His balance of Yin and Yang is a shining example of how we can all live life fully.

Also, this work is dedicated in loving memory to Professor William Chisolm, my mentor in Sports Medicine and in life. He was an innovator, councilor, healer, and a true teacher, pointing the way.

It is my hope that I, and all who learned from these men, will carry on the traditions of caring and healing as taught by their example.

And lastly, to my darling wife Michele, the light, love, and fire of my life. Thanks for your wisdom and guidance, and for being you.

Publisher
Acknowledgments

The publisher wishes to thank John Mutinelli for posing in the many exercise photographs. Thanks also to the Cathedral Oaks Athletic Club, Santa Barbara, California for allowing John to use their exercise equipment.

Special thanks to Ann Holms for her assistance with formatting and Linda White for her last-minute editing.

1

Overcoming chronic fatigue Syndrome – Healing Won't Come 'Til You Work For It

With life as stressful as it has been in the latter half of the twentieth century, and with all of the environmental and genetic pollutants we must endure, it's little wonder that many of us are chronically ill with diseases that force us to dramatically change our lifestyles. It's almost as if a safety valve went pop somewhere and the body said - enough, this is as far as the insanity goes. I need a rest!

The United States Center For Disease Control estimates that chronic fatigue effects some fourteen million citizens between the ages of seventeen and sixty-nine! Most of the victims are women (in fact, twice as many women as men). The Center For Disease Control in Atlanta suggests that women are 20 times more likely to develop chronic fatigue than breast cancer! (http://www.cdc.gov/ncidod/diseases/cfs/publicat.txt)

There is much conjecture as to why many of us are diagnosed with chronic fatigue Syndrome. Why do baby boomers have a disease previously unknown called Yuppie Flu? I believe I can explain. In this short piece, I'll tell you how I believe we got CFIDS (chronic fatigue Immune Deficiency Syndrome) and then I'll tell you what I did to remove the symptoms from my life.

In the 1950's, polio was the great crippler of children. There was no cure. If a child came down with the disease, he/she was assured of having some level of dysfunction, mild to massive, for the rest of his/her life. Some children even died from the dreaded disease. The drive was on to find a cure. When the Salk and Sabin vaccines were released, mothers rushed to have their children immunized. Within a decade, the only children who contracted polio were the ones who had adverse reactions to the inoculation. (The vaccine itself is still the major source of childhood brain swelling, encephalitis, today.)

Early on in the building of the anti-polio vaccine, there was a raging argument between Dr. Salk and Dr. Sabin. Dr. Salk believed that the serum needed to be made from an inactive virus so the child immunized would not contract polio from the shot. Dr. Sabin believed that true immunity could only be achieved if the body were sufficiently challenged. He used weakened but still active polio viruses in his inoculation to create antibodies in the child's body. At first Salk seemed to win the vaccine race. He was first, and it seemed to medical authorities that his notion was safer.

Due to a manufacturing defect, a batch of the Salk vaccine with fully active polio was produced and distributed. The results were tragic because hundreds of children were stricken with the disease. This was not seen as a failure of the manufacturing process but as a failure of the Salk principle, and as a result, the nation lost faith in the safety of the Salk vaccine.

Meanwhile, Dr. Sabin had released his drug. It was more convenient than the "shot" and much preferred by mothers who hated to "hold their children down" through the "needle" procedure. So the Sabin live vaccines in a sugar cube, or in drops under the tongue, became the treatment of choice for most of America's children.

For about four days after receiving the Sabin inoculation, children spewed polio viruses from every orifice. In other words, they were contagious as hell. Any non-inoculated child living with a recently treated youngster was likely to get polio (although these days it's classified as encephalitis so the vaccination statistics won't look worse than they are). But the problem progressed in time.

Unknown to medical science in the forties and fifties when polio was at its height, there was a continuation of the disease in those who carried the virus. Today it's called post polio syndrome, though many doctors still deny the existence of this disease.

Like the virus from chicken pox coming back to haunt a patient later in life as shingles, post polio syndrome is the result of being exposed to the polio virus. Mild encephalitis, muscle weakness, lethargy, extreme fatigue, muscle and joint aches, and a host of gastrointestinal, liver, and spleen complaints mark this syndrome.

Those who have had full-blown cases of polio as children usually have fairly bad bouts with post polio syndrome thirty to forty years later in life. But what about the rest of us who were given the live vaccine and have the virus lying dormant on the anterior horn cells of our spinal nerves? What happens to us thirty to forty years down the road?

The polio time bomb first exploded in a place called Incline Village, a ski resort in Utah. There, a significant number of "baby boomers" became ill with the same disease, all experiencing the above-mentioned symptoms. Since it was only affecting "baby boomers", and since medicine could find no cause for the complaints, the rash of sicknesses were brushed off as mass hysteria or some other psychosomatic condition and nicknamed the Yuppie Flu.

The Yuppies who populated this town were among the cream of the economic crop. They were all well-to-do high achievers with great paying jobs, high stress levels, and a love for physical activity. Since the sixties, the "baby boomers", had been burning the candle at both ends, passionately in favor of this cause or that cause, partying very hard, obsessively involved in their careers, and still trying to be super parents.

If any generation has loaded themselves down with decades of full-time stress, it's been the "baby boomers". Boomers' parents may have survived the great depression and WW II, but once those times were over, they allowed themselves to settle down and work quietly.

Boomers are different. They have stuff to prove. They could not let themselves turn into their parents. They had to make more money, they had to be liberated, they strived to have more possessions and status and on and on. They had tons of excuses for being excessive in nearly everything they did. Heap on top of that the constant bombardment of more industrial pollution and chemical insecticides than any other generation has ever endured! Add stress, the wear and tear of living, and pollution, and it's easy to see how their immune systems have become weakened to the point of failure. Enter the dormant virus.

Polio, like chicken pox, never quite goes away It just goes to sleep - sometimes for years. If chicken pox comes back with a vengeance as shingles when the immune system is weak, what happens to all those polio bugs that have bedded down in our spines when the thirty-year clock rings and we have a compromised immune system?

If you line up the symptoms side by side starting with mild encephalitis and working your way down the list, you'll see the manifestations of chronic fatigue and post polio syndrome are the same! The only symptom they don't share is the severe nerve exhaustion true polio patients have.

I knew I was in trouble when one afternoon in 1990, I temporarily lost the right half of my visual field. I could only see out of my left eye! Sitting at my desk while waiting for the next patient to come in, I peered across the room. My right eye was seeing only black with yellow zigzag lines. That, coupled with the headache and backache I was experiencing, and made me realize I had encephalitis. Although I never again lost my visual field, it was downhill from that point on.

After spending much time researching the cause of my ills and a good deal of time cooking up remedies with everything from herbs to electro medicine, the first incidental piece of information came my way.

All chronic fatigue immune deficiency syndrome patients tested had severely depressed sexual hormone levels. The men in their thirties and forties had testosterone levels of men in their seventies and eighties. It was the same for the progesterone levels of women in their thirties and forties.

Anyone who's been reading the anti-aging literature these days knows that sexual hormones are the fountains of youth and strength. As their levels decline, we age, become weaker, and lose potency, desire, energy, mental alertness, good moods, and muscle tone.

Many of the CFIDS patients have secondary infections such as mononucleosis (Epstein Barr Virus) and systemic fungal infections (usually the aftereffect of the overuse of antibiotics). The fungus in some was so bad that in two cases of CFIDS related deaths (which are rare), autopsies found fungus on the brain and floating around in the cerebro spinal fluid!

Now if there is EBV (Epstein Barr Virus) present, then, like mononucleosis, there would be a reduction in the number of nuclei in the cells and, more importantly, a decrease in the number of mitochondria, the energy engines of the cells.

The pieces of the puzzle were coming together. Enough, at least, for me to devise a treatment plan that would cover most of the bases. I needed to correct four problem areas, so the plan would have to include:

1. Something for the hormones.
2. Something for the virus.
3. Something for the fungus.
4. Something to reverse the loss of mitochondria.

But still something was missing. By this time I was working with a crowd of chronic fatigue patients. They were progressing, but still something else was needed.

That is when I noticed that most of them had what I euphemistically call a "piss poor attitude". Many of them held long-seated anger, and all of them had a deep resentment. This condition was putting a crimp into their ability to acquire material toys by curtailing their ability to work! Some patients felt that they were being knocked out of the work force altogether.

Many of the female patients had tried to be super moms – liberated working women caring for a family simultaneously with little space for any thing else in their lives. All of these folks, in the hustle of their three dimensional world, had lost their connection to their most important dimension - Their Center. They had forgotten that inside their bodies resided a soul!

During the time I worked with these patients, I noticed that only those who performed the physical / nutritional / medical routine had some improvement. In contrast, however, the ones who took the time to investigate and serve the yearnings of their spirit, to reconnect with their Center (the Creator, the Tao, God, whatever name you want to use), and who performed the physical / nutritional / medical routine... those folks were cured! It did not happen instantly, but it did happen. Six months to two years was the usual span of time.

There is no way to go back and undo the damage done by vaccinations, pollution, high living, or overwork. However, for those with chronic fatigue, here is a formula that will get you up and over the worst of it. All you have to <u>DO</u> is put in a GOOD deal of effort.

Every now and then when I overdo, i.e., go manic over home improvement, trade shows, teaching intensives (that's one semester's work taught in two days), too many radio interviews - I pay for it. But with a week or two of recovery and all of the recommendations below, I'm back on track again.

To those of you seeking a way out of CFIDS, put your heart into your own healing. Don't depend on others to heal you. It's your body - it's your job. As with most truly serious questions, the answers lie within us, waiting to be realized.

Author's Note:

As if to justify my belief that the polio vaccine has lead to CFIDS, there is now a move among some scientists and physicians to give chronic fatigue Syndrome a new and more appropriate name, Myalgic Encephalitis. This is the name the disease has always had in Great Britain. It is highly unlikely that anyone in the medical or government communities will ever admit to the truth concerning the cause of CFIDS. The issue of liability alone is too great. After all, the pharmaceutical cartel has conspired with the government on all levels, federal, state, and county, in order to create the pressure and coercion needed to infect our children. They are the ones who either knowingly or unknowingly forced the disease upon an unsuspecting public.

In medically forward-thinking countries, such as Japan, vaccines are at least optional. For parents wishing to vaccinate their children, the shots are only given after the child's second birthday, after the immune system has had time to mature. Maturity of the immune system is imperative. It is insane to overload the underdeveloped immune system with viral genetic material.

We are already seeing the consequences of such immune suppression on the general population. The challenges of childhood diseases are the stuff that naturally strengthens the immune system. The diseases come one at a time, not in batches of two or three different viruses at once! An infant's body cannot adapt to the extreme and sudden load!

It is my contention that children are being brain damaged and otherwise made sick by the vaccines and not from the diseases themselves! These drugs have also spawned a new set of diseases. I believe that autism, non-categorized before vaccinations, is an example of a disease created by the vaccination process. I also believe that officials of the pharmaceutical cartel not only know this but have asked for, and received, a ceiling to their liability in such cases from congress!

Comprehensive CFIDS Program

Nutrition and Dietary Supplements Daily

Vitamin C
2 to 5 grams daily. Or, just shy of having the runs.

Vitamin E
400 IU - 800 IU

Super Vit-a-Boost
(Multi Vitamin and mineral formula from Naturally Vitamins) 1 to 2 daily.

Any other supplements you may wish to take.

Supplements for Specific Actions

Aerobic O – 7
(Oxygen supplement – anti-viral, anti-bacterial, and anti-fungal)
20 Drops in a full glass of water or juice 4 times a day. (Manufactured by Aerobic Life)

Molybdenum
50 mcg. - 150 mcg.
Yeast can produce up to fourteen percent alcohol in your intestines from the carbohydrates that you eat. This mineral short circuits the process of alcohol production and keeps the fungus in chronic yeast infections from producing the alcohol that makes your brain swim and your mind dopey.

Wobenzym N
5 tablets 3 times daily in-between meals
This enzyme preparation acts as an anti-inflammatory and helps with the muscle and joint ache and swelling. It is also supportive of the liver, digestive and immune systems. AN ABSOLUTE MUST HAVE!!! This product is available from Naturally Vitamins of Scottsdale, Arizona.

Supplements For Men

Androstenedione:
• One 100 mg. capsule midday
• One 100 mg. capsule before bed

This supplement made from the Mexican yam plant converts to testosterone without lowering whatever you may already be producing. For the body to shut down its own testosterone production, blood levels of the hormone would have to be elevated for 12 hours + and then repeated for at least 3 days. Androstenedione only raises testosterone levels for three hours at a time, not long enough for the master gland (the pituitary) to notice. Your liver will take the supplement and begin to make testosterone out of the Andro within 15 minutes of ingestion! This should not be taken with juice or other acidic drinks as the Andro, sensitive to acids, is destroyed by them. Taking the Andro with a basic drink such as ginger ale will help to keep it active long enough to be absorbed.

Also available now is an Androstene cream that is meant to be absorbed through the skin. The rate of absorption of the Androstene via the cream is greater than that of the oral products. In addition, the cream has a blend of supportive and beneficial nutrients and herbs to both boost sexual function and muscle maintenance while keeping the testosterone produced from becoming Di Hydro Testosterone, which may injure your prostate, or from reverting up the hormonal ladder and becoming estrogen. No man needs estrogen. Not in any form, either naturally from isoflavones of soy or from insecticides. Studies are now pointing to the fact that increased sterility rates in men, and even prostate cancer, may be linked to estrogen instead of testosterone as previously thought. There are some 70+ studies to show that testosterone is not involved in prostate cancer and only 5 to suggest that it might be.

The Androstene cream (Andro – Edge) is available from Life Flo Health Care Products of Phoenix Arizona.

Supplements For Women

> **Progesterone Cream:**
> • Two applications as directed per day
> • 12 hours apart

This replaces the most needed hormone for women. All women need to read Dr. John Lees' book on women's hormones and menopause, <u>What Your Doctor Can't Tell You About Menopause</u>. Progesterone creams are available at health food stores nationwide. Good product names to look for are progesterone creams from Jason, KAL, and Life Flo.

Exercise

Use weight lifting to rebuild strength, muscular tissue, and to increase the number of nuclei and mitochondria in muscle cells. This will improve strength and energy overall. No other form of exercise will do, neither aerobics, dance, or Yoga. Nothing will accomplish the physiological goals stated but weight lifting. Period. The work needs to be conservative with most of the exercises being compound joint movements covering the largest muscles of the body with one or two exercises. Do no more than 3 sets of 7 to 10 repetitions of any exercise and give yourself a whopping 2 to 5 minutes in-between sets. Don't train like body builders. You have a different purpose in mind than beautiful biceps.

Strength training to improve the all-important Activities of Daily Living (ADL) must center around those structures that move and stabilize us, our central core, i.e., the thighs, pelvis, and torso. If these are worked, then everything else on the body will be improved. In time, after the central core strength improves, additional work that concentrates on the smaller muscles of the extremities can be done.

Find an exercise physiologist to guide you. Avoid personal trainers; they do not have nearly enough education to work with those who are ill. Work with sixty to eighty percent of your One Rep Maximum for each exercise. Increase the resistance routinely about every two or three weeks. Don't stay stagnant on a particular resistance level in any exercise. This part of the plan is the hardest for chronic fatigue patients to comply with. The fatigue seems too extreme. This is where you develop your willpower.

This workout utilizes the principles of Dr. Philip Rasch, one of the late deans of exercise physiology. Using the principle of compound joint motion, nearly every muscle in the body is worked using only a few exercises.

Find Your Spiritual Self

Now for the most difficult step. Don't get religious; seek God outside the dogma and greed found in most religions and "well established" spiritual teachers. Here is a rule of thumb that has worked very well for me – if they have fancy digs to pay for, leave. If they have lots of rules with do's and don'ts and we're the only ones, leave. Remember that God cannot be confined to buildings, dogmas, or sects. Neither priests, ministers, gurus, or your mother can dictate the truth of your relationship with the Creator. Search in whatever book or in whatever place your heart calls you to. Expect lots of twists and turns and dead ends in your search, but keep searching. Learn to trust intuition. (Guys this is the hardest thing for you. You must place the knowing of intuition with its data input from the subconscious over the reasoning power you usually use. As the Lama Lobsang Rampa wrote once: you are 9/10th subconscious and only 1/10th conscious. So why think with only 1/10th of your mind). Follow your heart, learn, learn, learn and then internalize that learning. At the Last Supper, Christ prayed we'd find the Oneness with God that he had acquired, that Oneness the ancients called Mystical Union. If you get on the road to finding it, The Creator will meet you halfway.

And there you have it. A simple program simply put. Be well, and have a speedy healing.

Sample Weight Training Program For CFIDS

Your weight training program should include the following exercises:

- **Leg Presses**

- **Back Extensions**

- **Pulldowns**

- **Crunches**

(See photographs on following pages)

Sample Weight Training Program

Leg Presses, 3 sets of 7

Figure # 1

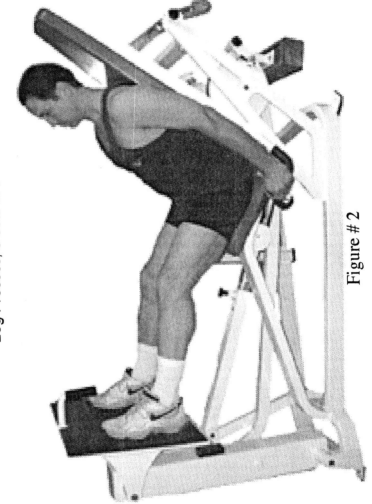

Sample Weight Training Program

Leg Presses, 3 sets of 7

Figure # 2

Sample Weight Training Program
45 degree Roman Chair Back Extensions
(Only to full extension - not to hyperextension)
3 sets of 7

Figure # 3

Sample Weight Training Program
45 degree Roman Chair Back Extensions
(Only to full extension - not to hyperextension)
3 sets of 7

Figure # 4

Sample Weight Training Program
Front Pulldown
(Palms facing you, hands shoulder-width apart)
3 sets of 7

Figure # 5

Sample Weight Training Program
Front Pulldown
(Palms facing you, hands shoulder-width apart)
3 sets of 7

Figure # 6

Sample Weight Training Program

Crunches

3 times max #'s possible per set

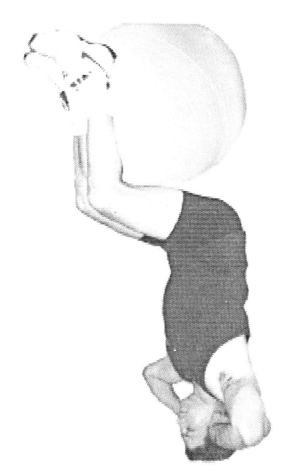

Figure # 7

Sample Weight Training Program
Crunches
3 times max #'s possible per set

Figure # 8

NOTES

NOTES

2

Fibromyalgia

Fibromyalgia is a disease of the nineties that's been around and misdiagnosed for a long, long time. Over three million Americans suffer from fibromyalgia today. Although fibromyalgia may be the older cousin of chronic fatigue, there is one major difference between the two diseases. While the manifestations are the same, you can get over chronic fatigue. It is highly unlikely that a patient will get over fibromyalgia. You can make things better... but there is just no getting rid of it completely.

Most of the victims of fibromyalgia are late middle-aged women. In the eighteen hundreds, women were told they had "hysteria" and should have their "hysti's" removed (hysterectomy) in order to "cure" the condition. In the sixties, these women (likely suffering from fibromyalgia) were fed tons of valium and sent home.

To this day the notion persists, especially among male "back-east" doctors, that there is a link between fibromyalgia and what used to be called female hysteria. If all of the painkillers, nerve depressants, and anti-depressants don't work, then these women must be crazy! As you'll see, none of the above mentioned medicines can ease the pain of fibromyalgia because they don't address the cause.

For the male victims of fibromyalgia, the stigma is just as bad. Since the fibrosis that's wrapping around the contractile tissue does not cause visible marks or make the face gray and drawn, the male patient looks just fine. "There's nothing wrong with you – you're just lazy. You're malingering ... you look fine ... get back to work". Many a male fibromyalgia patient has lost his job, his wife, and the understanding of his friends and family because – "He looks just fine"!

Whether directly related to CFIDS or not, the fatigue factor is just as bad. Add to that the nearly constant soft tissue pain, and it is nerve-racking to say the least. Yet, as with chronic fatigue, the patient looks okay; there are no obvious deformities, no glaring danger signals in the blood work. Aside from a slightly elevated white blood cell count, the usual battery of tests won't show any reason for the pain and disability. So, it must all be in your mind! How many times have fibromyalgics heard that one? And while there is a large psychological component to the disorder, it truly is a physiological disease. In many fibromyalgics, the psychological upset presents itself after so many physicians have discounted the extent of their pain and the depth of their weakness!

Since the fatigue component of CFIDS and fibromyalgia is almost the same, it's combated the same way. Let us look at the fibrous component of the disorder and see how we can set about remedying it. The fibro in fibromyalgia actually arises from the fibrous build up in the muscles of true fibromyalgics. (I say true because according to David Squires who headed the top fibromyalgia support group in the nation, more than half of the patients classified as fibromyalgics have been misdiagnosed. Allopaths are now using the diagnosis of fibromyalgia as a wastebasket term in much the same way they used the diagnosis of arthritis in the sixties and seventies. If they can't figure out what you've got, then it's fibromyalgia. " Here, take these anti-depressants, take these pain pills and go away.)

Science calls the problem an "over expression of fibrin". As part of the body's healing and maintenance mechanism, fibrin is laid down as a matrix for the formation of tissue around a wound or as connective tissue binding the intersection of muscles or tissues together.

When you are young and get cut either accidentally or from surgery, the wound heals cleanly with little scaring. Fibrin is deposited into the wound sparingly so that the tissue can grow through it. As we age (remembering that old age physiologically begins at 27), the system that deposits fibrin begins to go out of balance. Instead of being deposited into the wound sparingly, the fibrin almost totally fills the empty space, leaving little room for the tissue to grow through. This forms the thick, non-plyable scars we develop in our later years.

So it is with fibromyalgia that the system of laying down fibrin becomes further unbalanced and seeks to glue every moving thing down. When all of this stuff bears down on muscle bundles, it's a lot like sitting too long on the toilet - the blood supply to the legs gets cut off and ouch! The difference here is that the blood supply getting decreased now goes to the muscle. To add insult to injury, there is already a build up of necrotic debris in the microcirculation clogging up the tiny capillaries also occluding blood from these areas.

This process happens over years. Our blood not only carries oxygen and nutrients around, it also carries all of the toxins our system wants to get rid of. The toxins float around until they can reach the liver for deposition. The condition of the liver is essential. The toxins will keep floating around in the bloodstream until the liver can filter out the "crud"! Since most of us have clogged-up near-toxic livers, that bad stuff will be floating around the blood for a long time.

Tiny particles of debris go and clog the entrances to the tiny micro blood vessels. This action, while not life threatening, can impede overall circulation to an area. When this factor is added to the fibrous strangulation of muscle bundles, you can see how tissues can be screaming from oxygen starvation (Ischemia)! Here's where you get into the pain that conventional painkillers just can't touch.

Remember when you were a kid and just to see what would happen, you put rubber bands or string around your wrist and cut off the circulation? What happened? First, your hand went numb after turning an interesting shade of blue. Then it began to throb. If you tried to move the fingers or grip something, that throbbing turned into an ache ... a deep, deep, ache. That is the pain of Ischemia. Ischemia is also the cause of heart attack pain.

Aspirin, ibuprofen, and their cousins can't touch or alter such pain. Opiate medications can take the edge off. (Actually, they numb your brain, but the pain is still there.) Addiction levels among Fibro patients on these medications are extremely high. Non-Steroidal Anti-Inflammatories (NSAIDS), opiates, psychotropics, and central nervous system depressants are all part of the slew of drugs fed to fibromyalgia patients. The cure, in my opinion, is worse than the disease.

How did the body's repair system get out of balance? What is it in the young body that controls the over expression of fibrin? What controls the amount of necrotic debris in our blood when we are young? Why is the disposal of "crud" or detoxification more efficient when we are younger? A one word answer to all of these questions - Enzymes!

Age and stress cause the body's own production of enzymes to decline severely. When we get past twenty-seven years of age, we are working with a system in general decline. If left unchecked, by thirty-five years you will have had the most precipitous drop in conditioning and general health you'll ever face.

Exercise, even in the face of adversity and nutritional supplementation, can lessen that decline. Basically you can spread it out over fifty years instead of seven! But what about dealing with where you are now? The same cure applies: as long as there is breath, there can be improvement.

What's needed? Dr. Max Wolf discovered that a synergistic combination of protein-eating enzymes sparked the body's production of its other enzymes. If you supplement vitamins, which as co-enzymes are helpers to the enzymes, does it not make sense to supplement the enzymes themselves?

For fibromyalgia, the Wolf enzyme formula, Wobenzym N, has three very important actions:

- It eats excessive fibrin.
- It eats necrotic debris.
- It helps the white blood cells.

Research has shown that in wound repair, dealing with scar tissue, fighting fibrotic build up in the breasts and in muscle tissue, Wobenzyms' fiber-eating enzymic action balances the system without going overboard in the opposite direction. These enzymes eat necrotic debris in the blood stream and open up microcirculation. This action improves overall blood flow.

This preparation also helps the white blood cells do a better job for the immune system. White blood cells are the soldiers and the trashmen of the immune system. These blood cells envelop an enemy and then tear the critter asunder with little hands called FC receptors. After killing the bug, the white blood cell then carries around the left-over pieces until it can get rid of the trash. Here the liver is involved again, and the slower and more toxic the liver is, the longer it takes to clean the FC receptors.

The Wobenzym N enzymes eat the junk from the FC receptors, freeing the cells from being garbage men and returning them faster to their roles as soldiers. All of these actions and uses have been proven in over 160 peer-reviewed, mostly double blind studies of the product. No other nutritional supplement is as well backed up by science.

Okay, so now you've freed up the circulation around the soft tissue by taking enzymes and exercising. (Follow the exercise plan laid out for the chronic fatigue patients in Chapter I.)

What else can be done? You can combat the reduction in the tissue stores of Andenosine Triphosphate (ATP) caused by the localized Ischemia. ATP is the energy on which all of your body runs. When you are low on ATP, the muscles not only ache, they can incur damage if the depletion lasts long enough. The damage produces more fibrotic deposition as a scaring response. A vicious cycle begins. Even after blood flow is restored, it may take up to seventy-two hours for the muscle stores of ATP to be recharged. Enter Ribose. This rare sugar can supercharge the process of replenishing ATP, reducing the time from seventy-two hours to twelve hours and then maintaining better levels of ATP than are normal for a Fibro patient.

It is now recommended that heart attack patients be given Ribose immediately after the episode to prevent further damage to the heart muscle. Ribose replenishes the ATP in much less than seventy-two hours after the infarct. It works just as well on skeletal muscle as it does on the heart muscle. Creatine should also be taken along with the Ribose to improve ATP production in muscle tissue. This is the combination that "hard charging" athletes use to rebuild their energy stores after incredible workouts. Your muscles certainly deserve the recharging that theirs do!

The Ribose and Creatine both serve to quickly replenish ATP in the muscles. Then Magnesium is needed to overcome spasming muscles. (Calcium controls muscle contraction and magnesium controls relaxation. Muscles cannot spasm in the presence of enough magnesium.) Malic acid helps the body produce ATP; Molybdenum keeps any systemic yeast infections from producing mind-clouding alcohol in your intestines. Vitamin C builds immunity and helps keep blood vessels and connective tissue glued together. The Wobenzym N in the daily formula is both for its anti-inflammatory properties and its anti-fibrotic functions.

Folks on this program should expect to feel different within three to six weeks, although beginning a resistance exercise program may produce a bit of soreness, the body will get used to the workout in three to four weeks.

Of special concern to me is my observation that about half of the female fibromyalgia patients that I studied were very angry with their lives. Most of these women were hard charging professionals who put their work, knowingly or unknowingly, ahead of their relationships with their husbands and children. Some of them were too busy to have children. Then, at the end of their careers they looked around; their beds were empty, no one was present to call them mom or grandma, and most of the accomplishments of business seemed to pale in the face of not having a family around to love them. Although sexist sounding, this seemed to be their experience.

Fibromyalgia in these patients is the somatization (physical expression) of the soul's pain. (Please don't confuse this with psycho-somatic illness; it's not all in your head. What I'm saying is that the body expresses the deep hurts and the grief we carry around.) This realization reflects a decade of intense work with many, many fibromyalgic patients. Involving oneself with caring work, giving lovingly to others while being mindful of one's limitations, and not pushing the physical exertion too far serves to lessen the pain and lighten the load.

Fibromyalgia patients need to avoid being around other sick people, not from fear of contamination, but from the reduction of life force that is "sucked" away by those who sit around complaining incessantly about their ills. Look for love, but also seek every opportunity to give love away.

Comprehensive fibromyalgia Program

Nutrition and Dietary Supplements Daily

Ribose
5 gms. (One teaspoon)
Mix in juice or water and drink four times a day

Creatine
5 gms. (One teaspoon)
Mix in juice or water and drink four times a day

Magnesium
400 mg. capsules
One capsule three times a day with meals

Malic Acid
500 mg. capsules
One capsule three times a day with meals

Molybdenum
50 mcg. to 150 mcg. capsules
One capsule daily

Vitamin C
500 mg.
Three to four times a day with meals

Wobenzym N
5 tablets three times a day in-between meals

Super Vit-A-Boost
Multivitamin and Mineral from Naturally Vitamins
One tablet a day with meals

If the symptoms of extreme fatigue are also present, then overlap this with the CFIDS Program in Chapter I.
EXERCISE!

NOTES

NOTES

3

Lower Back Pain

Man has probably had back problems since the first human walked upright. We, as a species, are not yet fully adapted to bipedal locomotion, and the weak spot in our structural system is the lower back.

Every year nearly two and one half million Americans suffer injuries on the job and forty-seven percent of those workers have incurred lower back injuries ranging from mild sprains to herniated discs (U.S. Department of Labor, Bureau of Labor Statistics. For internet users URL: http://www.bls.gov/). Add to that number the thousands who hurt themselves doing housework, gardening, exercising, and the like, and you can see why lumbar and pelvic trauma form the largest classification of injuries.

When you stand, the entire weight of the torso and head rest on the few little lumbar vertebra and their discs. The intervertebral discs are like shock absorbers. They can be likened to jelly doughnuts with hard fibrous exterior coatings on the outside and sacs with a jelly-like substance on the inside. As you step, jump, or move, the vertebra squish down onto the discs. If the force of the movement is spread out along the spine, then no one disc has to take all of the force. But if, as so often happens, you concentrate that force on a particular segment of the spine, not allowing for dissipation, the compressive energy is then multiplied in one or more spinal segments. This causes the "jelly" to burst out of its enclosing sac and press out against the spinal nerve trunks. Ouch!

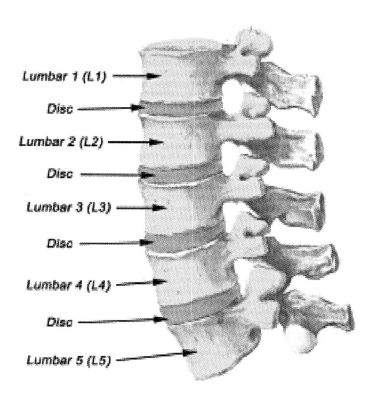

Not only will you have pain but you will also lose some function. The weight of a dime on a spinal nerve trunk (the spot where the nerve comes out from the spine) will decrease the conductivity of that nerve by up to fifty percent. It's like having only half the possible electricity going down a wire and into a light bulb. The light bulb won't burn very brightly. So, whatever body parts are affected by the decreased conductivity of the spinal nerves won't work well until the pressure is alleviated.

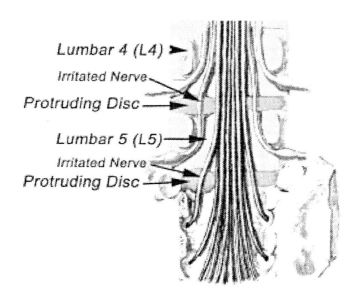

Lumbar 4 (L4)
Irritated Nerve
Protruding Disc
Lumbar 5 (L5)
Irritated Nerve
Protruding Disc

For example: A herniated disc at the L5/S1 level will cause pain down the front of the thigh and the side of the leg while decreasing the ability of the penis to attain full erection for the male. In time the body will desiccate (dry out) the disc and thereby relieve the pressure, but that may take up to two years.

Surgery is touted as an answer, but I don't believe it is. Sixty percent of the back surgeries performed fail. Sixty percent of those surgeries must be performed again. Sixty percent of back surgery patients will have more pain post op than they did before the cutting! (Calodney, A., Failed Back Surgery Syndrome. Burton, A.K., Prediction Of The Clinical Source Of Low Back Trouble, Using Multivariable Modules. Spine, 16: 7-14. 1991. Walker, B.F., Failed Back Surgery Syndrome, Journal Of The Australian Chiropractic & Osteopathic

Association. Volume 1 #1, 1992) My opinion is that if you can avoid back surgery at all, avoid it! There are alternatives that I will address later in this chapter.

Another source of lower back and pelvis pain comes from the sacroiliac joints. It's been known since 1885 that these joints, located where the spine meet the pelvis, are semi-moveable. (A.T. Still, founder of Osteopathic Medicine, proved the SI joints to be semi-moveable instead of fixed in 1885.) Conventional (allopathic) medical science has taken one hundred years to discover what most undergraduate anatomy students already knew. Semi-moveable joints can slip out of their notches, stretching ligaments, and biting down on soft tissue creating a crippling pain in the back and hip.

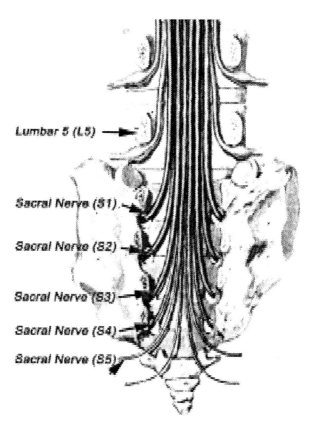

Lumbar 5 (L5)

Sacral Nerve (S1)

Sacral Nerve (S2)

Sacral Nerve (S3)

Sacral Nerve (S4)

Sacral Nerve (S5)

All lower back conditions begin with bad bio-mechanics. Most people lift, stoop, reach, and twist improperly, and we all tend to stand improperly.

There are two muscles in the pelvis called the Iliacus and the Posas Major. These structures run from the inside aspect of the lower back vertebra (the lumbars) and also from the inside of the pelvic basin. They travel down and inside towards the top, inside of the thighbone. The muscles' primary action is to flex the hip, as if you were knee kicking someone directly in front of you. In babies, these muscles are short, due to the fact that the infant has been curled up in the fetal position during the gestation period. When the baby begins to crawl, the ilioposas is stretched. The longer the child crawls, the more this muscle gets stretched.

If a baby is made to stand and walk too soon, these super-tight muscles will not stretch adequately. As a pre-teen, the child will stand with the fanny backwards like a duck (anterior pelvic tilt), giving him/her a condition known as lordosis. This lordotic posture squeezes the discs of the bottom three vertebra, pinching them at their rear aspect and forcing the liquid to the front. With age, weight, and wear, it may only take a twist or a small load to make that jelly bulge or fully pop out of its disc thereby creating all sorts of pain and problems. This malposition in standing also aggravates the sacroiliac (SI) joints as shearing forces are placed upon them, forcing them to move out of position.

Aggravating any lower back condition from a full blown herniated disc to a simple fascia (connective tissue) strain are four sets of muscles that react badly to any type of insult. The muscles are:

• Ilioposas group
• Quadratus lumborum
• Piriformis
• Iliotibial band

During the period of injury, muscle spasms build from mild to severe in order to force you to limit the range of your movements. They form the natural splinting mechanism for back injury. It is really good that the back is splinted against movement and further insult, but you hurt like crazy when these guys are in spasm!

The piriformis, for example, lies across the back of the pelvis deep under the buttocks. It lies right over the sciatic nerve. When the spasm occurs, it bites down on the nerve, causing pain to radiate down the back of the thigh and into the calf and foot. But the sciatic nerve has two branches, the tibial and the collateral; pain can be felt in the side of the thigh as this branch goes to the iliotibial band. So, you wind up with a combination of pains from spasm and nerve pressure!

With so many structures involved, one can see that caring for low back and pelvis pain is not a simple thing. This is why the allopathic mode of treatment - painkillers and muscle relaxers - is sheer nonsense. Mechanical problems DEMAND a mechanical solution. If the front end of your car is out of alignment, squeaking, and causing you to lose the ability to steer, pouring oil on it would be ridiculous! The squeak would quiet the components down but would do nothing to correct the misalignment. It is this complete lack of biomechanical education that makes MD's think that mechanical problems can correct themselves. If mechanical reduction is demanded for other conditions like dislocated joints or fractures, then why ignore subluxations (partial dislocations) of the SI joints or vertebra?

SI joint displacement, if caught early, is easily remedied by manual manipulation (Chiropractic, Naturopathic, or Osteopathic adjustment). In my opinion, the physical therapy techniques of bone manipulation emerging now are not as effective as the Chiropractic, Naturopathic, or Osteopathic schools of manipulation.

SI joint subluxation that has been treated allopathically and allowed to remain "out of joint" is much harder to correct because the body perceives this area as unstable and attempts to calcify the area shut. When this happens, there is no way to move the SI back in place. This will cause everything from nearly constant backaches to whopping headaches.

The sacrum forms the bottom pump for cerebro spinal fluid respiration. The sphenoid and occiput bones at the floor of the brain form the top of the pump. When you breathe, these cranial bones tee-ter-totter against each other at their meeting point in the center bottom of the skull. This action pumps brain fluid around the brain case and down the spinal canal. Again, when you breathe, the sacrum (the triangular bone at the base of the spine) rocks minutely front to back pumping the fluid back up.

When the bottom pump doesn't work because one SI is jammed, the entire cerbrio spinal fluid pump is backed up. After back injuries or from being out of joint for prolonged periods, the SI joints tend to calcify shut. Orthopedists then use injections of cortisone into an SI joint to cause localized osteoporosis and prevent the joint from calcifying shut. (I've had to have one of those done; it hurts like hell!)   Mechanically caring for a subluxation early keeps lots of nasty things from happening to you.

When it comes to herniated or bulging discs, alternatives should be considered before surgery. There is a Chiropractic method called Cox Distraction Technique which draws the protruding nucleus pulposa (jelly) back towards the disc. It's impossible to suck the stuff back into the disc, but it is possible to move it back away form the nearby nerves, relieving a good bit of the pain. With time, the body reabsorbs the jelly permanently relieving the pressure. In 1986, when I had a herniation of a lumbar disc, I coordinated my orthopedic and chiropractic care. After my initial visit to the MD, I hobbled into my DC's (Doctor of Chiropractic) office, walking with my hands on my knees for stability and to alleviate as much pain as possible. After the Cox Distraction work, which is gentle ice and microcurrent electro therapy, I walked out of the office straight up ... and with a lot less pain.

With the care received from both of my physicians and my own blend of nutrition plus rehabilitative exercise, I went from having one of the worst disc herniations my orthopedist had seen in 30 years of practice to recovering full function, full range of motion, and nearly full strength in eight weeks!

Your body needs the proper supplements to:

• Relieve inflammation
• Reduce swelling
• Speed healing in the injured area

During the time of intense pain and spasming, you need to reduce the inflammation present in the epithelial and connective (soft) tissues surrounding the affected bony segment. If you can reduce the inflammation, the body will significantly reduce the pain. This is accomplished safely and without side effects with Wobenzym N - used in Europe for forty years, with over one hundred sixty scientific studies to verify its effectiveness and absolute safety, Wobenzym N is the alternative to toxic anti-inflammatory medication. Enzymes are substances the body uses to produce over six thousand needed reactions.

As you age or come under stress, the body's own production of these enzymes is depleted. When the protein eating enzymes of Wobenzym N are supplemented, the body's own production of enzymes begins to cascade. During trauma, enzymes have been shown to reduce inflammation while greatly speeding repair. When inflammation is reduced, the body does not have to send out its pain signals. The pain of an injury or condition is relieved without needing an analgesic.

During times of injury, a patient should take twenty Wobenzym N immediately on an empty stomach. Then ten tablets three times a day for as long as the high level of pain persists. Why so many? Enzymes are huge things and you can only fit so much in a pill. The folks at Wobenzym N know that senior citizens make up a large segment of the customer base using the product. Wobenzym N keeps the tablet small and slick so that older folks can easily swallow it. Olympic athletes in Europe are familiar with this overloading routine, called Stoss Therapy. After the acute period of the injury is over, take the average dose of Wobenzym N, which is five tablets three times a day.

This wonderful preparation will do everything from helping clean out your arteries to strengthening your blood vessels, preventing varicose veins. It will also heal soft tissue and help with digestion. Vitamins, which are actually co-enzymes, may each perform four to six different functions. When taken systemically, enzymes perform thousands of different functions.

Along with the enzymes you need to supply the building blocks of tissue to aid in the repair process. The back is braced with a stringy supportive material called fascia. Those of you who have dressed out livestock or game are familiar with the fascia that holds the skin on the muscles and the patch of deep fascia on the backs of animals. Most of us are familiar with the white stringy stuff that holds the peal onto an orange. All that is fascia. We all have a hexagon-shaped area of fascia from our lower ribs to the crest of the pelvis. This material holds everything underneath in place. When you strain the back, aside from the muscular and ligament injury, you tear this fascia. Of all of the tissue in the body, fascia is perhaps the slowest to heal. This is partially due to the poor blood supply going to these areas and partially because our diets lack the one nutrient building block fascia is composed of – sulfur. Sulfur is to fascia what calcium and magnesium are to bone. Our diets are woefully poor in sulfur.

A century ago, mothers would give their kids a tablespoon of black strap molasses with a pinch of old black gunpowder on it. This mineral rich combination gave their children plenty of sulfur (both from the black powder and molasses). It provided iron and B vitamins. The saltpeter from the gun powder kept teenagers out of sexual escapades.

Today, we have an easily available source of sulfur in the product MSM. Veterinarians used this supplement first to help race horses rebuild fascia torn in heavy training. During the injury, 1000 mg. of MSM should be taken daily. Afterwards, a 500 mg. dosage should be taken for maintenance.

Next you need the glue that holds connective tissue together and that is simple old Vitamin C. Your daily C intake needs to be in the gram and not milligrams range. We are among the only mammals that cannot make our own Vitamin C. The goat, for example makes about seven grams of Vitamin C per one hundred pounds of body weight daily. That's 7000 mg.! The FDA's recommended daily requirements may be fine to keep a two-ounce lab mouse disease free, but you weigh substantially more. An adult's daily ingestion of Vitamin C should be at least 1000 mgs. (one gram) or just shy of having the runs.

Nutrients are needed to control spasms and must be taken daily. They are the building blocks tissue's need to repair the affected areas and are required so that the process of restoration can begin.

The Nutrients

We need to address the nutritional needs of the muscular tissue involved. Muscle is part of the family of epithelial tissue. This epithelial family includes skin, eyes, the internal organs (especially the reproductive ones), and the muscles. The building block for all of these is zinc. In order to repair itself properly, the body needs 100 mg. to 150 mg. of zinc; 50 mg. to 75 mg. daily is a good maintenance dose of zinc after the repair process has been completed. The maintenance dosage will keep the eyes, female organs, and men's prostate happy. With the addition of 400 IU to 800 IU of Vitamin E and 10,000 IU of Vitamin A, you've got all of your tissue repair nutrients covered.

Finally, you need lots of Magnesium. Muscular contraction (the electrical impulse to tighten the muscle) is governed by calcium. To release the muscular impulse, magnesium is needed. When a spasm hits and stays, it indicates that the muscles are low on magnesium. In the office, natural doctors often do what's called an IV push of up to 2 grams (2000 mg.) of magnesium for patients with all kinds of sustained involuntary contractions from menstrual cramps to back spasm. An IV push means that an intravenous needle is placed in a vein and a medication injected directly into the bloodstream for immediate use in the body. At first these patients experience some flushing and mild nausea but in twenty minutes or less the spasm and its pain are completely gone! You can take between 1200 mg. and 1600 mg. of Magnesium to assure that you are covered against any spasms that may occur during the healing process.

Mental Focus and Attitude

Most folks of the old school expect that healing will come to them with no effort on their part. They do not have to will it, think about it, or lift a finger for it. Those folks are part of the population that was told to constantly expect medical miracles. Medicine will find the cure for every ill and one day even put an end to death. In my opinion, that is one big lie made to keep folks under the control of doctors and the pharmaceutical cartel. Medicine may be able to keep your body living in certain circumstances, but what about the quality of that life?

The quality of the healing that occurs in allopathic back patients is poor. Compared with those folks who have put effort into their recovery, the passive folks are not as strong or nearly as able. The effort needs to come from being an active part of the treatment plan - not from blindly following the orders of supposed experts just because someone said that they were experts.

Formulating a supplement program to augment your body's healing, visualizing the results you expect your body to attain (notice I did not say hope for), and, most importantly, exercising very hard to attain that degree of mobility and strength will bring success. A back injury without exercise is only patched up and never healed. Pain is no excuse to avoid exercise. There is a level of exercise for every level of ability.

Now, let's begin a program of nutritional and progressively harder stretching and strengthening to limber up shortened and spasmodic muscles. Shore up those areas and prepare to return to the normal performance of your activities of daily living (ADL's).

Comprehensive Lower Back Program

Nutritional and Dietary Supplements

Immediately after injury	During acute pain	Maintainence
Wobenzym N 20 tablets	Wobenzym N 10 tablets 3 times daily in-between meals	Wobenzym N 5 tablets 3 times daily in-between meals
	MSM 1000 mg. daily	MSM 500 mg. daily
	Zinc 100 mg. to 150 mg. daily	Zinc 50 mg. to 75 mg. daily
	Vitamin C 1000+ mg. daily	Vitamin C 1000+ mg. daily
	Vitamin E 400 IU to 800 IU daily	Vitamin E 400 IU to 800 IU daily
	Vitamin A 10,000 IU daily	Vitamin A 10,000 IU daily
	Magnesium 1200 mg. to 1600 mg. daily	Magnesium 1200 mg. to 1600 mg. daily

Exercise

There are three stages to the exercise program based on the level of pain and the ability to move.

STAGE ONE:　Movement is painful and difficult
STAGE TWO:　Movement is less painful and difficult
STAGE THREE:　Body is sore while movement is easier

Each stage is demonstrated in the two categories of stretching or strengthening. Most people don't mind stretching but hate the strength work. However, doing one without the other is like putting a new tire on your car and then neglecting to screw the bolts onto the wheel. A flexible back without strength will be unstable and injury-prone. A strong but inflexible back will break under a load. The combination of flexibility and strength is what is needed to complete the work of healing.

All of these things - nutrient supplementation, exercise, and mind set will put you in control of healing your lower back and pelvic pain. Don't expect the recovery to be fast; be satisfied with steady. The blood supply to the lumbars is poor and that, combined with having to use it every day even though it's hurt, means that the process of recovery and rebuilding is a slow one. But if my example means anything – I thought during my recovery that I would never again be able to lift heavy weights, something I love to do. I have been lifting again these past many years since the injury, along with teaching martial arts and being fully active. I expect an occasional bout of pain for a few days from doing something stupid (like the time I moved a fully laden 5 x 8 foot bookcase), but for the most part, I am pain free and, most importantly, surgery free!

Note: Men over 50 years of age with persistent lower back pain that does not react to any type of direct lower back therapy need to be checked for prostate cancer. Many times a cancerous prostate will produce an unrelenting backache as the disease travels up the spine. Don't guess, don't deny, and don't take chances – get it looked at.

Sample Training Program For Lower Back Pain

Your training program should include the following exercises according to stage of pain and movement.

STAGE ONE	STAGE TWO	STAGE THREE
Movement is painful and difficult	Movement is <u>less</u> painful and difficult	Body is sore while movement is easier
Hip Roll Stretch Version 1 (Stretching)	*Hip Roll Stretch* Version 2 (Stretching)	*Hip Roll Stretch* Version 3 (Stretching)
Single Knee Williams Version 1 (Stretching)	*Single Knee Williams* Version 2 (Stretching)	*Single Knee Williams* Version 3 (Stretching)
Seated Toe Reach Stretching as far as is comfortable	*Seated Toe Reach* Stretching as far as is comfortable	*Seated Toe Reach* Stretching as far as is comfortable
Prone Torso Extension Version 1A (Strengthening)	*Prone Torso Extension* Version 1B (Strengthening)	*Prone Torso Extension* Version 4 (Strengthening)
Prone Torso Extension Version 2A (Strengthening)	*Prone Torso Extension* Version 2B (Strengthening)	
Prone Torso Extension Version 3A (Strengthening)	*Prone Torso Extension* Version 3B (Strengthening)	
Crunch Sit-Up Version 21A (Strengthening)	*Crunch Sit-Up* Version 21B (Strengthening)	*Crunch Sit-Up* Version 21B (Strengthening)
Crunch Sit-Up Version 22A (Strengthening)	*45 Degree Roman Chair* Version 1 (Strengthening)	*45 Degree Roman Chair* Version 2 (Strengthening)
Crunch Sit-Up Version 23A (Strengthening)		*Crunch Sit-Up* Version 23B (Strengthening)

(See photographs on following pages)

How To Perform The Exercises

STAGE ONE: Movement is painful and difficult

Hip Roll Stretch Version 1
Lie face up on a bed or floor. Keeping the shoulders flat on the bed turn your hips as shown, so that they are at a 90 degree angle to the shoulders. Bend the hip to 90 degrees, then bend your knee to 90 degrees. Now rotate your knee down towards the floor or bed. You'll feel this stretch at the waist, lower back, and buttocks.

Single Knee Williams Version 1
Lie face up on a bed or bench. Grasp one knee in both hands and draw that knee up towards the chest. Take the stretch up to the first point of pain and hold. The non-working leg is flat on the bed. On this one, you're stretching the hamstring, buttocks, and lower back muscles on the side that's up.

Seated Toe Reach
Sit on the floor with the legs straight ahead of you. Place your hands at your knees and then walk your fingers down your legs as far as you can go. Remember: take a stretch only to the first point of pain and hold there. As you progress that first point of pain will happen further and further down into the stretch. Keep your knees flat on the floor. When you get to the furthest point you can go, grab onto you shins and count. Progress further and further down until you can reach past your toes.

Prone Hyperextensions Versions 1A, 2A, 3A (Pick a version of the exercise that fits your ability level.)
Lie face down on the floor with your hands by your sides. Slowly raise your head, chest, and shoulders 4 to 6 inches. Breathe out while you move. Hold for a second, then slowly return your chin to the floor.

Crunch Sit-Up Versions 21A, 22A, 23A
Lie as shown and hold your hands on the front of your thighs. When you crunch, reach for the bottom of your kneecaps bringing your head, chest, and shoulders up 4 to 6 inches from the floor.

Stage One Stretching
Movement is painful and difficult
Hip Roll Stretch - Version 1

Figure # 9

Stage One Stretching
Movement is painful and difficult

Single Knee Williams - Version 1

Figure # 10

Timeless Voyager Press

Stage One Stretching
Movement is painful and difficult
Seated Toe Reach

Figure # 11

Stage One Strengthening
Movement is painful and difficult

Prone Torso Extension - Version 1A
(pillow under hips and torso only, hands at side)

Figure # 12

Stage One Strengthening
Movement is painful and difficult
Prone Torso Extension - Version 2A
(same with hands at chest)

Figure # 13

Stage One Strengthening
Movement is painful and difficult

Prone Torso Extension - Version 3A
(same with hands in front)

Figure # 14

Stage One Strengthening
Movement is painful and difficult

Crunch Sit-Up - Version 21A

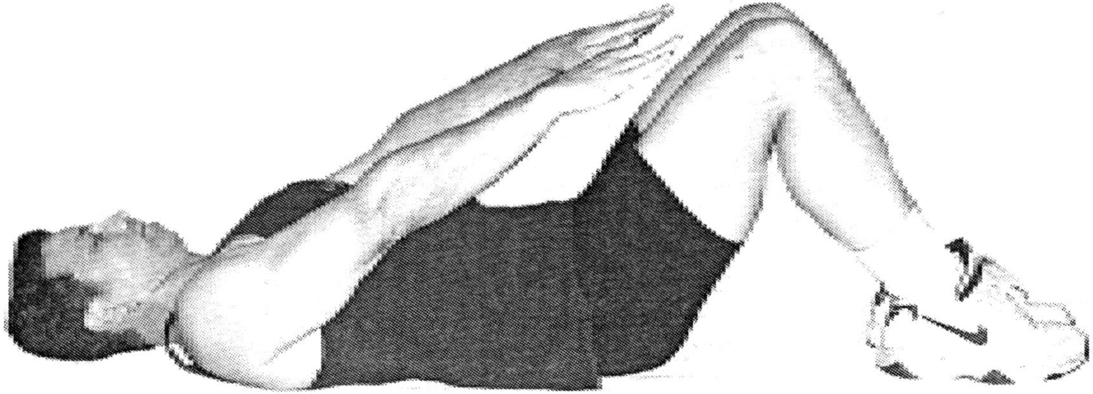

Figure # 15

Stage One Strengthening
Movement is painful and difficult

Crunch Sit-Up - Version 22A

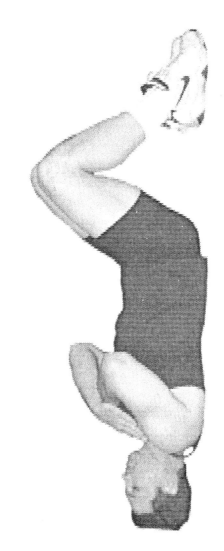

Figure # 16

Stage One Strengthening
Movement is painful and difficult

Crunch Sit-Up - Version 23A

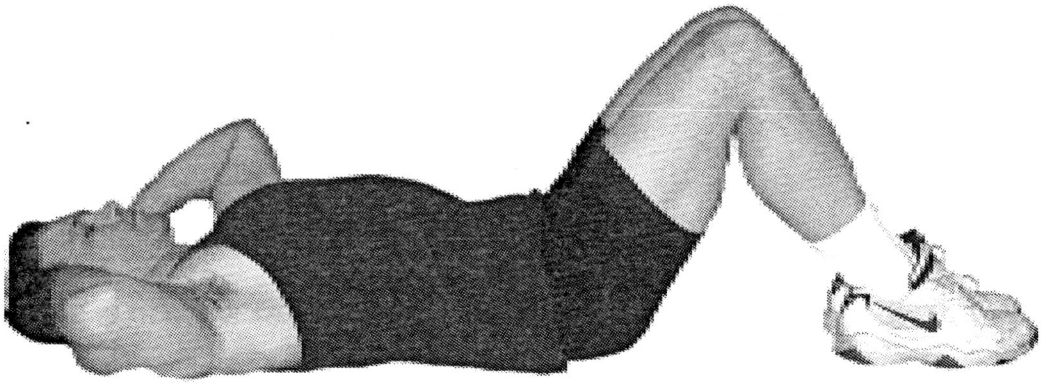

Figure # 17

How To Perform The Exercises

STAGE TWO: Movement is <u>less</u> painful and difficult

Hip Roll Stretch Version 2
Lie face up and stretch as you did before, but this time bring the working leg over the edge of the bed. Let your foot dangle down towards the floor. This time you'll feel the stretch more in the piriformis muscle under the buttocks.

Single Knee Williams Version 2
This time begin with both legs dangling off the edge of a bed or bench as shown. As before, grasp one knee in both hands and draw up as far as you can. The important side on this version of the stretch, though, is the one that is down. That extremity is stretching the ilioposas muscles where the thigh meets the pelvis.

Seated Toe Reach
(See instructions for Stage One)

Prone Hyperextensions Versions 1B, 2B, 3B (Pick a version of the exercise that fits your ability level. After a month of work at that level, progress to the more difficult movement.)
Hold your hands under your chest. This time draw your knees up 4 to 6 inches as well as the head, shoulders and chest.

Crunch Sit-Up Versions 21B
Hold your hands under your chest. This time draw your knees up 4 to 6 inches as well as the head, shoulders, and chest.

45 Degree Roman Version 1
Secure yourself on the bench and trust it to hold you up. Fold your arms over your chest while hanging. Bring your torso up so that the shoulders feel in line with your knees. This is full extension. Do not arch back into hyperextension as this can compress the rear portions of the interveterbral discs. This wonderful exercise can also be used as a stretch if you allow yourself to hang forward at the starting position of the exercise. Stretching like this will open up the interveterbral articulations and decrease pressure on the nerves.

Stage Two Stretching

Movement is less painful and less difficult

Hip Roll Stretch - Version 2

Figure # 18

Stage Two Stretching

Movement is less painful and less difficult

Single Knee Williams - Version 2

Figure # 19

Stage Two Stretching
Movement is less painful and less difficult

Prone Torso Extension - Version 1B
(pillow under hips and torso only, hands at side)

Figure # 20

Stage Two Stretching

Movement is less painful and less difficult

Prone Torso Extension - Version 2B

(same with hands at chest)

Figure # 21

Stage Two Stretching

Movement is less painful and less difficult

Prone Torso Extension - Version 3B
(same with hands in front)

Figure # 22

Stage Two Stretching
Movement is less painful and less difficult
Crunch Sit-Up - Version 22B

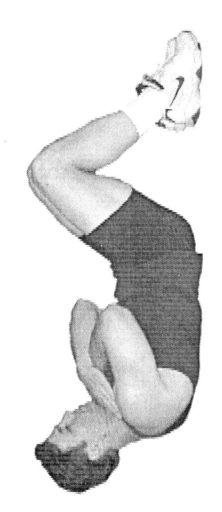

Figure # 23

Stage Two Strengthening
45 degree Roman Chair Back Extensions
Version 2
(Only to full extension - not to hyperextension)
3 sets of 7

Figure # 24

Stage Two Strengthening
45 degree Roman Chair Back Extensions
Version 2
(Only to full extension - not to hyperextension)
3 sets of 7

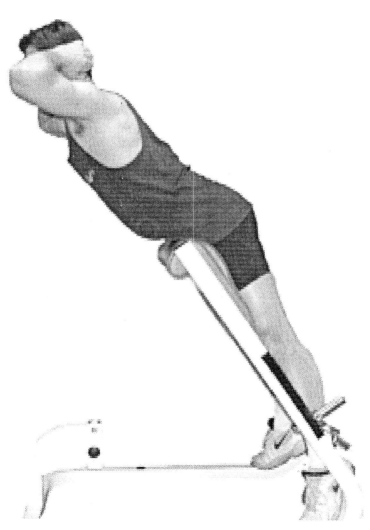

Figure # 25

Timeless Voyager Press

How To Perform The Exercises

STAGE THREE: Body is sore while movement is easier

Hip Roll Stretch Version 3
In this version, allow the foot to dangle more towards the floor. This intensifies the stretch of the piriformis muscle at the buttocks and of the iliotibial band muscle at the side of the thigh.

Single Knee Williams Version 3
This stretch is done as before but now you should be flexible enough to draw the knee all the way back towards the chest while leaving the opposite side dangling.

Seated Toe Reach
(See instructions for Stage One.)

Prone Hyperextension Version 4
Keeping your arms straight out in front of your head, raise the torso and thighs.

Crunch Sit-Up Versions 22B
Clasp your hands behind your neck and hold the elbows out to the sides. Now raise your chest and shoulders taking the head along for the ride. Cradle the head and neck in the hands. Do not yank on the head and neck to raise your shoulders, as this will cause neck strain. Don't give yourself another injury.

45 Degree Roman Version 2
Hold the hands behind your neck as with the sit-up. Whenever you go to the harder version of this or any strength exercise, decrease the repetitions done and build up to the prior high number again over time. When you become stronger still, you can hold a dumbbell up against the chest to increase the resistance during the work.

Stage Three Stretching

Body is sore while movement is easier

Hip Roll Stretch - Version 3

Figure # 26

Stage Three Stretching
Body is sore while movement is easier
Single Knee Williams - Version 3

Figure # 27

Stage Three Stretching

Body is sore while movement is easier

Prone Torso Extension - Version 4
(same while lifting knees also)

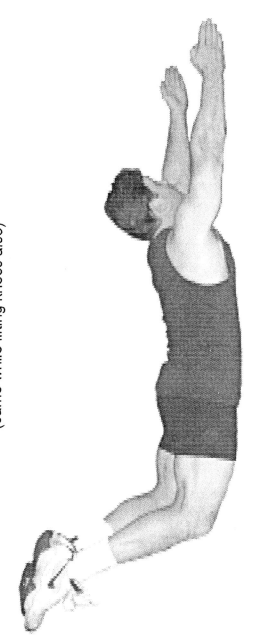

Figure # 28

Stage Three Strengthening
45 degree Roman Chair Back Extensions
Version 2
(Only to full extension - not to hyperextension)
3 sets of 7

Figure # 29

Stage Three Strengthening
45 degree Roman Chair Back Extensions
Version 2
(Only to full extension - not to hyperextension)
3 sets of 7

Figure # 30

Stage Two and Three Stretching
Body is sore while movement is easier

Crunch Sit-Up - Version 21B

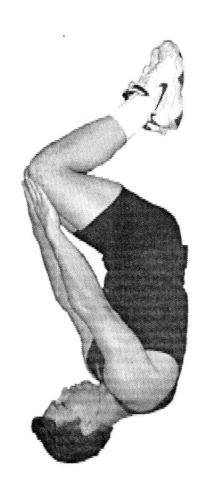

Figure # 31

Stage Three Stretching
Body is sore while movement is easier
Crunch Sit-Up - Version 23B

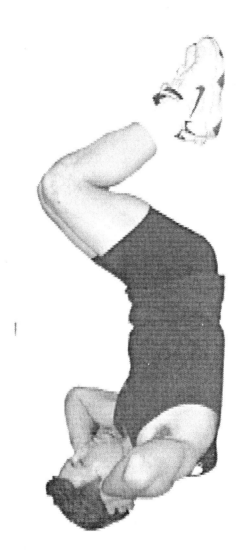

Figure # 32

NOTES

4

Mid Back Pain

Increasingly, people in all professions are coming down with pain in the mid back. Not limited to particular walks of life, this painful condition is experienced from mom's to physicians. The area between the shoulder blades and just below has become a focus of pain for many. Why does this pain arise? Why is it there? What can you do to get rid of it? Let's look at the anatomy in order to understand what causes mid back pain.

The thoracic vertebra are the primary bones of the mid back and to either side of these are the ribs. Just over the ribs are the wing bones (scapulae), onto which our arms attach. The free moving scapulae are unique among bones because they are literally floating, their only connection to the torso via their attachment to the collarbone (clavicle) and its connection to the sternum. Lacking a real bone to bone connection, the scapulae are held in place by the structures that move them - the scapular stabilizer muscles.

While many muscles arise from the scapulae, most go to the upper arm and form the rotator cuff. The only muscles that attach from the spinal column to the scapulae are the Rhomboids, connecting from the inner border of the scapulae to the spinal column. The mid Trapezius lies over the inner border of the bone and the scapular spine moving inward and downward and finally attaches to the spinal column. If you take a look at the average mid back, you'll notice that most people have a hollow between their shoulder blades. That hollow is not supposed to be there - muscle tissue is missing!

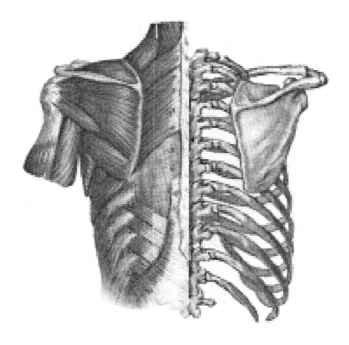

Spinal malposition is most common among the people of developed countries. Kyphosis (rounded shoulders or, in extreme cases, dowager's hump) is not a natural phenomena. People become that way due to incorrect posture. Leaning over to do schoolwork, kitchen work, desk work, some sports, and even martial arts can cause this spinal malposition.

Being bent forward like that restricts rib cage expansion and inhibits taking in a full breath. Kyphosis throws our posture forward placing a strain on the lower back and stabilizer muscles that are attempting to hold us upright. The malposition causes our arms to rotate internally at the shoulder joint. This places a strain at the rear of the shoulder joint. Over time it produces a laxity in the supportive ligaments allowing easy dislocation of the shoulder. The posture looks ugly! Man was not meant to look like his stoop-shouldered, knuckle-walking cousins, the apes.

Finally, the part of the ribs that articulate with the spinal segments tend to dislocate slightly (sublux) every now and then. Even though it's not a full blown dislocation, a subluxed rib can be extremely painful. That is because the soft tissue in the surrounding area swells and presses on little nerve endings creating enormous pain!

What can you do to overcome this malposition and the pain it brings? First, you must ameliorate, then remediate. The swelling, pain, and spasm must be addressed in order to allow for work, both your ADL's (activities of daily living) and the work of exercise. Severe pain in this area is usually a sign of rib subluxation. It should be looked after by a physician, expert in manipulative therapy. (A chiropractor or naturopath is my choice.)

Adjustment usually brings instant relief, though the side effects of the subluxation (inflammation) must still be addressed. The precipitating factors that allowed for the subluxation to occur in the first place (muscle imbalance) must also be addressed. In cases of trauma, tennis back swing, golf follow-through, or some other movement, begin examining the possible strain, sprains, or even fractures. A qualified physician is needed in order to make the right assessment.

Okay you've done all that and you still have the mid back pain - here is my plan:

First, you eliminate the physiological basis of the pain. For this you reduce the chemistry of inflammation and spasm by taking five tablets of Wobenzym N three times a day in-between meals. When the pain dies down, which may take weeks, you can maintain the 5/3 dose or drop down to three tablets, two - three times a day.

Since muscles cannot spasm if enough magnesium is present in the tissues of the body, I suggest 1200 mg. - 1600 mg. daily of magnesium to support enzyme functions while decreasing the possibility of spasms. It's impossible to overdose on magnesium because it is the most important mineral for bio-physiological functioning! Constantly in use, constantly at loss, constantly in demand.

Because you'll be rebuilding tissue soon in the exercise / rehab phase, zinc is the primary mineral building block of epithelial tissue. Zinc: 50 mg. - 75 mg. daily. And finally, an eyedropper of Body Mend (Rio Energetics) every 3 to 4 hours. This homeopathic medication calms down the body's reaction to trauma. (It has also been found helpful for PMS and menstrual pain.)

Next, eliminate the biomechanical basis of the pain. That hollow in-between the shoulder blades means that your mid back muscles haven't enough strength to carry your upper body through your day. The paraspinal muscles of the spine are overworked trying in vain to hold your torso up while the rhomboids and mid–trapezius are too weak to help much in pulling the shoulders up. They are already having a hard enough time moving your scapulae and arms through your daily work. Overwork equals pain. The cure is hard exercise.

Comprehensive Mid Back Pain Program
Nutrition and Dietary Supplements Daily

Wobenzym N
5 tablets, 3 times a day in-between meals
3 tablets, 2 - 3 times a day (maintenance)

Magnesium
200 mg. - 1600 mg. daily

Zinc
50 mg. - 75 mg. daily

Body Mend (Rio Energetics)
One eyedropper every 3 to 4 hours

Exercise Program For Mid Back And Shoulders

- **Pulldowns**

- **Dumbbell Rowing**

- **Seated Rowing**

- **Upright Rowing**

- **Arm Across Stretch**

- **Hanging Chin Up**

(See photographs on following pages)

Mid Back and Shoulder Routine to be done twice a week.

Front Pulldowns
• 3 sets of 7 - 10 repetitions

Grasp the bar with the palms facing you with hands shoulder-width apart. Using a reverse grip (palms away from you - also known as pronated) and pulling down either in front or behind the neck can create shoulder injuries in those much over 27 years of age. The chin up grip described is a better exercise biomechanically than the pull up grip. It's better at saturating the back and arms with exercise since it provides almost twice the range of motion of the pronated wide grip version.

There are two major principles for creating a proper strength training movement: 1) The body segment likes to be worked in its primary range of motion. 2) The body segment likes the fullest range of motion it can complete.

The chin up grip fills these two biomechanical requirements the other grips and angles do not.

When beginning resistance exercises, find the maximum weight you can lift. Do the movement once (one rep max). Then take 70 % of that weight and do at least 7 repetitions during each set. Try to add one repetition to the set each consecutive week until you've reached 10 reps per set.

The following week, add 5 to 10 pounds to the resistance and decrease the repetitions to 7. Work your way back up again. That means that you'll be on a specific weight for about three weeks before you increase the challenge to your body. Always be working at increasing the intensity of your exercises. Any time you allow a weight or a number of repetitions to be stagnating over a period of time, your progress will also stagnate.

Using this multi-faceted approach, supplementing specific strengthening, and stretching, you will be targeting the culprits of this nagging and physically limiting pain.

Mid Back Pain Exercise Program
Front Pulldown
(Palms facing you, hands shoulder-width apart)
3 sets of 7-10

Figure # 33

91

Mid Back Pain Exercise Program
Front Pulldown
(Palms facing you, hands shoulder-width apart)
3 sets of 7-10

Figure # 34

Mid Back Pain Exercise Program
Bent Over Dumbbell Rowing A
3 sets of 7-10

Figure # 35

Mid Back Pain Exercise Program
Bent Over Dumbbell Rowing B
3 sets of 7-10

Figure # 36

Mid Back Pain Exercise Program
Seated Rowing with Machines or Cables A
3 sets of 7-10

Figure # 37

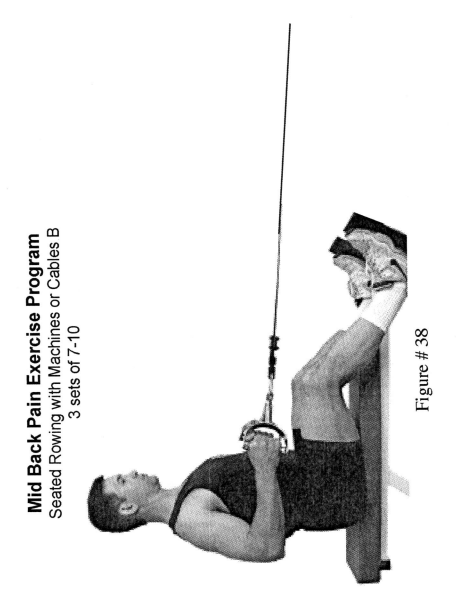

Mid Back Pain Exercise Program
Seated Rowing with Machines or Cables B
3 sets of 7-10

Figure # 38

Mid Back Pain Exercise Program
Barbell Upright Rowing A
3 sets of 7-10

Figure # 39

Mid Back Pain Exercise Program
Barbell Upright Rowing B
3 sets of 7-10

Figure # 40

Mid Back Pain Exercise Program
Arm Across Stretch
3 times, 30 seconds per hold

Figure # 41

Timeless Voyager Press

Mid Back Pain Exercise Program
Hanging on Chin Up Bar
3 times, 30 seconds per hold

Figure # 42

NOTES

NOTES

5

Fibrocystic Breast Disease
Systems Out Of Balance

Thirty to forty percent of premenopausal women will get cystic mastitis (fibrocystic breast disease). The symptoms of this condition can vary widely. Feelings of mild congestion to severely painful inflammation of the breasts is very common. The primary cause of the fibroid cysts in the breast, as well as in the uterus, is a level of estrogen in the body that is too high.

Increasingly, the word estrogen is becoming linked with another word – Cancer. High estrogen levels have been found to increase the likelihood of getting breast, uterine, and cervical cancers. Yet in typical allopathic logic, estrogen is prescribed to women for the treatment of these same problems!

One horror story about estrogen was told to me by a young woman who was the victim of a hysterectomy. After finding uterine fibroids, the young woman's OBGYN put her on estrogen therapy. Within a month her fibroids had grown exponentially and she was rushed into an emergency surgery to remove her uterus. To this day her doctor (a woman also) disputes any connection between estrogen and the growth of fibroids!

The great fear for most women is that fibrocystic breast disease can be a precursor to breast cancer. There is, however, a little known study all women should be aware of.

Over the course of five years, an extensive study was conducted in Germany on 247 patients to establish the fiber eating properties of systemic enzymes. (#1. Scheef, W, Gutartige Veranderungen Der Weiblichen Brust. Therapiewoche [1985], 5090. #2. Scheef, W, "Neve Aspekte In Der Kompleten Behandlung Von Tortgschiritten Malignen Tumdreen", In Mediziniscne Enzym-Forschungsgesellshaft e.v. [ed]), Systemiscne Enzymtherapie, 3rd Symposium, Vienna, 1988.) The ability of enzymes to eat away at excessive fibrin in tissues has been widely studied and well known. This data, however, had only been applied to controlling the growth of excessive scar tissue post operatively and eliminating the fibrous matrix that forms arteriosclerotic plaque responsible for clogging arteries.

Oncologists in both Europe and the United States have been using systemic enzymes for years to eat away at the fibrous outer coating of cancer cells. This procedure allows medications and the body's own cancer killer cells (tumor necrosis factor, interleukins, etc.) to get in and kill the cancerous cells. It wasn't until 1985 that anyone thought of using the fiber eating properties of systemic enzymes to treat fibrocystic breast conditions.

The 247 women were divided into two groups. In the first group, 124 women received a dose of 10 Wobenzym N tablets twice a day while the second group of 123 women received 10 Wobenzym N tablets plus 1000 mg. (IU) of Vitamin E daily. Doctors evaluated the patients' progress using sonographic examination along with self reporting of tenderness and pain.

After the first six weeks, 65% of the women in the Wobenzym N <u>only</u> group and 85% of the women in the Wobenzym N plus Vitamin E group were free of complaints. Many of the women had a complete regression of the disease!

This study sparked a double blind study of Wobenzym N vs a placebo on 96 women. A profile of each woman was taken. Her levels of pressure and pain were evaluated while a sonogram recorded the number and size of the cysts every two weeks. There was no significant reduction in the size and discomfort level of the 96 women receiving the placebo in contrast to the women receiving Wobenzym N. The Wobenzym N group had significant reductions in the number and size of their cysts! After the conclusion of the study, women who stopped taking the Wobenzym N preparation had the symptoms return. However, supplementing with Wobenzym N again relieved the condition.

The famous work of Dr. John Lee has made women aware of the role of estrogen in promoting disease. Too much estrogen and not enough progesterone is the basis for many of the diseases women now experience. We are constantly exposed to substances that mimic estrogen in our bodies, according to the world's leading environmental allergist, Doris Rapp M.D. Dr. Rapp points out that common chemicals in insecticides, industrial pollutants, and fertilizers find their way into our bodies. These common toxins all mimic estrogen and are ruining the hormonal balance of both women and men. This process is made much worse by the allopathic insistence on prescribing estrogen for the various ills that women experience in their reproductive organs or cycles.

As a part of any treatment for fibrotic conditions in women, progesterone cream should be used. Dr. Lee prescribes an application of the cream be applied both morning and evening at least twelve hours apart. This restoration of an essential hormone to a woman's system reduces the size and painfulness of the cysts. According to Dr. Lee, the enzyme and nutritional supplementation can control or eliminate the condition completely.

Since progressive fibrocystic breast disease can lead to cancer, Wobenzym N may be valuable in keeping the condition from worsening.

Fibrous deposition is a process balanced by the enzymic functions of the body. The balancing mechanism is thrown off because of a lack of enzyme production due to age and stress. You need enzymes to make enzymes.

In general, I've noticed that women who seem to be more susceptible to fibrotic disorders (fibrocystic breast disease, uterine fibromas, and fibromyalgia), have diets lacking in live, enzyme rich,

Timeless Voyager Press

foods. Fresh uncooked vegetables and fruits are live, enzyme rich foods and should constitute a large portion of the daily diet. When cooked, canned, or processed, vegetables and fruit lose their enzymes, they still have some nutritive value but they do nothing, however, to support the body's enzymic processes. Dietary changes and supplementation with enzymes, are of great value in preventing fibrotic conditions.

Supplements For Women

Wobenzym N
Ten tablets, 2 times daily

Vitamin E
1000 IU Daily

Progesterone Cream
One dab twice daily twelve hours apart. It's cheap insurance.

NOTES

Timeless Voyager Press

NOTES

6

Erectile Dysfunction

The first best selling pharmaceutical in the world is an antidepressant, but the second is a deadly medication to enhance erections! (My publisher has insisted that I do not name the medication due to possible legal matters; however, the first letter is "V".) The result of this medication is an erection; however, one of the negative side effects is stroke or heart attack. Now, some men would be willing to risk having a stroke or heart attack in order to have an erection, but I will introduce a less risky alternative which can produce the same results in a healthier way!

Erectile dysfunction is a problem faced by some twenty million men. Although all men, for various reasons, will have some "failures" in achieving full erection periodically, erectile dysfunction isn't limited to those in their senior years. Eighty percent of the problem happens to men under sixty-five! For most men, facing declining erectile ability due to aging, the problem can be corrected most of the time using natural substances and exercise.

Erection medications only address a portion of the physiological issues facing men with the problem. A comprehensive program of supplementation and exercise can bring out the best in a man. Let's review what the problem is and what can be done to address the situation. If you're lazy or want an easy answer to all of life's problems, then don't bother reading any further – take the drug and play "erection" Russian Roulette. If, however, you don't mind increasing your health and strength while you get your friend working again, then please follow along.

The chicken or the egg. Which came first? As men progress in years, they have the usual enzyme depletion and the decline in function that it brings. First, little things stop working, then big things begin to happen. A lack of enzymic action in the body happens due to one's age, stress, and a diet lacking in live foods. Usually though, it is a grand combination of all of the above.

Lowering the body's production of enzymes allows the over-production of fibrin which forms the matrix of arteriosclerotic plaque in the arteries blocking blood supply to various parts of the body including the pelvis. After the age of twenty-seven, when physiological old age hits the male body, function begins to decline. In other words, sexual hormone production begins to wane and by thirty-five most men report a decrease in the size of their erections.

What causes the decrease in the size of the erection? Boredom with their sexual partners? In some instances, yes. Circulatory insufficiency in the pelvis and lower extremities (LE)? That's more likely. Add to that a decline in testosterone after age forty or so and you've got a deadly combination for satisfactory penis function.

Autopsy studies during the Vietnam War showed that the young troops already had up to a forty percent blockage in the arteries of their hearts. If those arteries were blocked, then you can bet that all of the other arteries were just as occluded! If there's a forty percent blockage at nineteen, then what's it like at forty, fifty, or sixty? The chances are very strong that the trend continues - and probably at an increasing rate!

Knowing the basics of the physiological problem, I have created a plan to overcome erectile dysfunction. First, you need an agent that will gently eat away blockages (plaque) in the arteries and then eat the debris that is clogging the microcirculation to tissues. If you've read the preceding chapters, you know the answer already. Wobenzym N.

If it seems by now that Wobenzym N is the closest thing to the "magic bullet," you're right. A vitamin can create or enhance up to a dozen different functions. Every vitamin and mineral is a co-enzyme - something that helps enzymes to work. This enzyme combo sparks the body's own production of the 2000+ other enzymes, which, in turn, create thousands of enzymic reactions! Now, in order to aid in the reduction of cholesterol build-up on the plaque, add lecithin to the tune of one tablespoon of the granules a day.

Overcoming the hormonal decrease is a bit more difficult. That all starts in the pituitary gland just under the front of your brain. The pituitary gland secretes a substance known as a luteinizing hormone (LH). LH travels down to your testicles via the bloodstream and tells them to produce testosterone, the testosterone, in turn, — well, you know the drill from here.

If you have a doctor who is an anti-aging expert or endocrinologist, he may inject you with LH or testosterone. Of the testosterone's available, the synthetic testosterone, *methyl testosterone*, can damage the liver and cause liver cancer. The natural testosterone, *cypionate* (made from bull testicles) is much less likely to cause damage. Since the cost of each is comparable, in my opinion, the health-conscious individual should opt for the natural one.

There are supplements that use only substances found occurring naturally in plants and animals, and a near match to LH is found in the plant Tribulus Terrestris. The Tribulus from Bulgaria is the strongest and most well processed. Velvet Dear Antler, a Chinese medicine used for centuries, also provides an LH like substance.

These are golden days for men with hormone problems because many testosterone replacements are available over the counter. The most popular testosterone replacement with the sports crowd is Androstenedione. When taken as I direct, Androstenedione will have the effect of dramatically increasing the blood levels of testosterone.

My directions will keep the pituitary gland from thinking that there is too much testosterone around and shutting down its LH production. This way you can make more of it on your own, plus have a boost.

Testosterone improves overall mood, fights depression, increases libido, improves erectile ability, and maintains/improves muscle and bone mass. After age fifty, most men lose ten percent of their muscle mass each year. By sixty, you can be down to a bare-bones minimum muscle mass. It does not have to be that way! That change is directly linked to the decrease in testosterone. Androstenedione can help.

In order to help the Wobenzym N do its job of opening micro-circulation, I will include a program of exercise at the end of this chapter. But you still need more supplements.

Two great supplements are directly related to increased blood flow during erections: Yohimbe and Di Methyl Glycene! Yohimbe is from the inner bark of the African tree of the same name. In some West African tribal societies, Yohimbe is used to spark mass fertilization rituals, a stew is made from the bark and ingested by every adult in the tribe.

Yohimbe is noted for its vaso dilatation of the blood vessels in the pelvis and for its effect on the brain and central nervous system in stimulating sexual activity. For an over-the-counter preparation, Yohimbe has no equal. The most potent extract I recommend is *Twin Labs* Yohimbe Fuel. I believe it works very well. Yohimbine HCL is sold as a pharmaceutical and works wonders when taken thirty to sixty minutes before sexual performance. You'll need a doctor's prescription for that one!

Di Methyl Glycine is an amino acid that very few know anything about. Used on horses for almost three decades, and in Eastern Europe, it is an anti-impotency agent that dates back to the seventies. DMG (Di Methyl Glycine) has a way of increasing the circulation to the pelvis and lower extremities. It was first noted when veterinarians used the amino acid on horses to aid the recovery from exercise.

Male horses would achieve enormous erections when given DMG. A full reference to DMG, how it works, and the politics surrounding its sale in the U.S. can be found in Dr. Morton Walker's book, Sexual Nutrition. DMG is available for human use in the U.S. as Tri Methyl Glycene or Betaine (not Betaine HCL).

DMG is converted by the body into some very useful substances. For example, the B vitamin, Choline, which the brain uses to make the neuro transmitter, Acetyl Choline. As you age, your production of neuro transmitters declines and you need to feed a steady amount of precursor nutrients to the brain to maintain its proper functioning.

The amino acid, Arginine, when taken alone in fairly large doses increases the production of seminal fluid and sperm. Since it converts into citruline, and that converts into nitric oxide, it is used as an erection enhancer. Increasing the formation of nitric oxide is what the "V" drug is supposed to do. Arginine will do that and more without the side effects. This level of Arginine has been thought to act as a Human Growth Releaser and thus seems to help with any anti-aging program.

Lastly, let's not forget the most essential nutrients for sexual function, Zinc and Vitamin E. All of your internal organs, muscle and eye tissue are made of Zinc. Zinc is to epithelial tissue as calcium is to bone. The largest storehouse of Zinc in the body is the prostate gland. With every ejaculation, you lose a large amount of Zinc and Vitamin C. The body easily restores the C, but the Zinc is another matter.

We are one of the most Zinc-deficient societies in the world. Unless you eat a bushel of oysters, whole wheat, or half a cow, you don't have enough Zinc in your body. The 15 mg. daily recommendation from the FDA may be enough to keep a two ounce lab mouse from getting a swollen prostate, but a man can lose more than that amount of Zinc every time he achieves orgasm!

Every case of a swollen prostate, regardless of what it turns into later, is the result of a Zinc and Vitamin E deficiency. Alcohol abuse and promiscuity also add to the problem.

Back in the sixties, Dr. Thomas K. Cureton, University of Illinois and dean of all exercise physiologists, discovered that Vitamin E was essential to sexual function. There is an interesting story that goes along with that discovery. Another professor at the university, who disliked Cureton, sought to prove his conclusions wrong.

The professor recreated the study using a heat processed wheat germ oil and, of course, did not get the same results (vitamin E is destroyed by heating). He then called Cureton a fraud. A year long battle ensued between the two. The last shot of that battle was fired when Cureton "stole" the professor's wife - and married her. See, Vitamin E did work!

All of the supplements in the world won't do a bit of good unless they can get to the areas where they're needed. So, let's get this good stuff to where you need it most – your pelvis. In rehabilitation, we know that if you can increase the blood flow to an affected area you can bring nutrients to that spot, healing it faster.

Exercise holds the key to increased blood flow to the pelvis. Wobenzym N can eat away at blockages and open microcirculation. The DMG can create its vaso dilating effect. The LH can get to the testicles. And the Andro gets to do its job too. Get my message? Exercise holds the key to circulation. The horses would benefit from the effects of DMG as long as they were well trained and had good circulation! Consider this muscle building for your most important muscle (which is actually a gland).

Lower Extremities (LE) and Pelvis Program

Principle: Resistance exercise increases the vascularization of a muscular structure by forty percent. That means a forty percent increase in the size of existing blood vessels and a corresponding forty percent increase in microcirculation of new blood vessels. We will apply this exercise physiology principle to bringing more fresh blood to your pelvis and lower extremities.

This exercise program is not etched in stone; if you have exercise equipment, use it. What is presented here is a bare-bones basic outline requiring little or no gear. Perform these exercises 3 to 4 times a week, maximum. Exercise is a stimulus and response mechanism. For every session of stimulus, you need the body time to respond. If you pile too much exercise on your body, the immune function suffers. If that routine is kept up for too long, as with endurance athletes, you'll get sick and possibly die young (as many of them do). Over-exercising has become so prevalent with the overachieving boomer generation that there is now a journal for exercise and immunological medicine.

Note:

There are books and programs available that cover direct exercise for the penis. Since there are three muscles in and around the area that can be strengthened, thickened, and made to hold a better "pump," penis exercise should not be laughed at. Also the spongy open structures that fill with blood during erections can, like our joints, organs, and muscles, be restricted by fibrosis.

Any of our internal organs can become fibrotic much the same as do the muscles. It's that fibrosis that restricts us from touching our toes (when the hamstrings become tight or turn into kidney fibrosis, Glomerulosclerosis). When scar tissue (fibrosis) forms inside the spongy cavities (as it does to all men with aging), it restricts the expansion of the penis when the body tries to fill it with blood. Judicious penis exercise and use of a vacuum pump will help. Please note I said judicious. Remember that the penis is a delicate appendage, so don't overdo it. Any good thing taken to extremes will have negative results. Your cure may be worse than the original disease! Read the data, study the books. If you need to, talk to a urologist. Many of those physicians are even prescribing penis vacuum pumps now!

Comprehensive Erectile Dysfunction Program

Nutrition and Dietary Supplements Daily

Wobenzym N
10 tablets, 2 to 3 times daily in-between meals

Androstenedione
One (1) 100 mg. - 150 mg. capsule mid afternoon and one (1) before bed with a basic drink (ginger ale), and without food.

Alternate **Androstenedione** Therapy

Androstenedione Cream
Androstenedione creams now available. They have better absorption and utilization than the oral supplements. There is an herb called Crysin that prevents the testosterone your body will make from turning into the female hormone estrogen. It will not convert into the prostate damaging hormone DHT (though now science tells us that it's actually the conversion into estrogen that seems to be hurting the prostate and not the testosterone per se). This cream is made by Life Flo company of Phoenix Arizona.

Arginine
3 - 6 grams Daily
NOTE: The powder is the best form of this supplement to use. One teaspoon is equal to 3 grams (3000 mg.) This should be mixed with water or juice and taken between meals especially before workouts, and just before bed on an empty stomach. The powder is available from NOW.

Zinc
75 mg. to 100 mg. daily

Vitamin E
800 IU daily

Betain or **TMG**:
1500 mg. daily

Yohimbe:
2 capsules daily, in-between meals
or one hour before sex.

Tribulus:
750 mg. daily

NOTE: For those men with high blood pressure due to kidney damage or dysfunction, check with your physician before using Yohimbe. While Yohimbe is used to lower blood pressure in those with high peripheral resistance to blood flow, it can be hard on those with kidney-caused high blood pressure. Use the herb *Maca* instead.

How To Perform The Exercises

Exercise Program for LE and Pelvis

Recumbent Cycle

Pedaling for 12 to 24 min. at moderate to heavy resistance, 3 times a week. Aside from being a great heart exercise, this work, at higher levels of resistance, serves to build and strengthen the muscles of the pelvis and thighs thereby increasing circulation overall. A recumbent bike is preferred because regular cycle seats are known to cause inflammation of the internal sexual apparatus and can cause sterility. In countries such as Holland, where much cycling is done, as many as twenty percent of the men have sexual or reproductive dysfunction.

Freehand Squats

With the feet shoulder-width apart and your toes and knees pointed out some 40 degrees. The hands are held at the hips, the head looks up at a point above the wall. Do 3 sets of 20 to 100, depending on your strength. If you start at 20, add 5 reps per set per week until you get to 3 sets of 100. By then you should be looking for leg press equipment.

Flutter Kicks

Lie face up on the deck with the hands just under your hips. Now, do an abdominal crunch by bringing your head, shoulders, and chest up. Hold this position to tighten the upper abdomen. Raise both legs 8 to 12 inches from the floor. Alternately kick each leg up 12 inches without letting the feet touch the floor. Do 3 sets of up to 200. If you want to go for time, kick for 30 seconds a set to start with, then add 15 seconds to each set per week. Work up to the point where you can do 2 minutes or 200 kicks.

Crunch Sit-up

3 sets of up to 200. Keep the lower back flat on the floor. Bend the knees and hips to 90 degrees of angle each. Hands are behind your neck, elbows out. Do not pull on the neck to get the body torso up! Lift from your shoulders and take your head along for the ride, cradled in the hands.

Exercise Program For LE and Pelvis
Recumbent Cycle
Pedaling for 12 to 24 min. at moderate
to heavy resistance, 3 times a week

Figure # 43

Exercise Program For LE and Pelvis
Freehand Squats A
3 sets of 20-100

Figure # 44

Exercise Program For LE and Pelvis
Freehand Squats B
3 sets of 20-100

Figure # 45

Exercise Program For LE and Pelvis
Flutter Kicks A
3 sets of up to 200

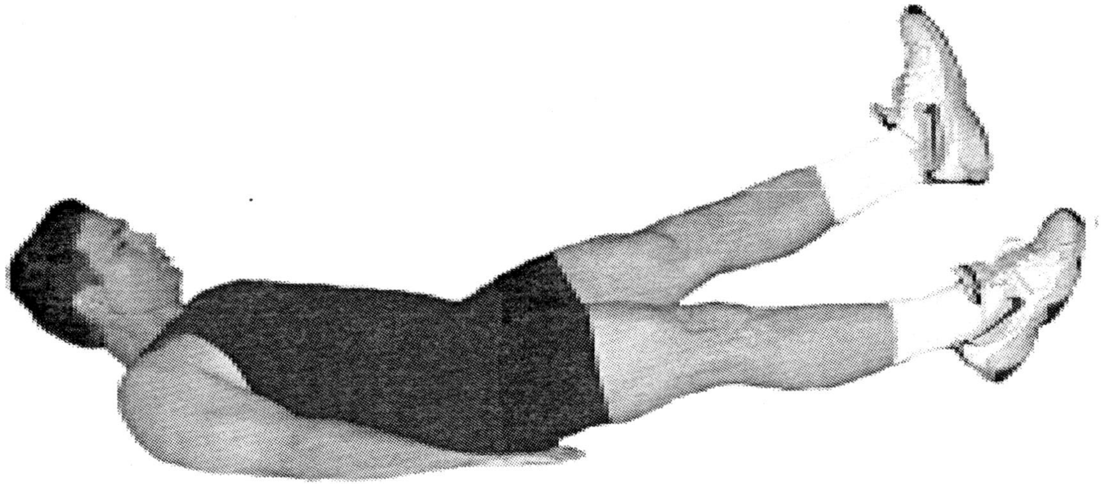

Figure # 46

Exercise Program For LE and Pelvis
Flutter Kicks B
3 sets of up to 200

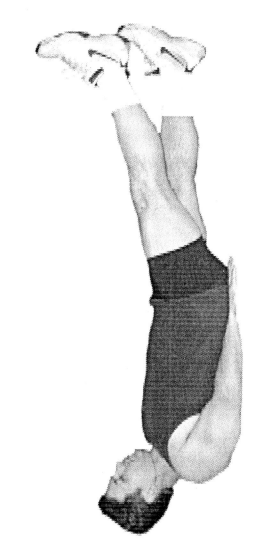

Figure # 47

Exercise Program For LE and Pelvis
Crunch Sit-up A
3 sets of up to 200

Figure # 48

Exercise Program For LE and Pelvis
Crunch Sit-up B
3 sets of up to 200

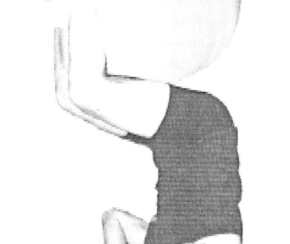

Figure # 49

NOTES

_____

_____

_____

_____

_____

_____

_____

_____

_____

_____

_____

_____

_____

_____

_____

_____

_____

_____

_____

_____

_____

_____

_____

_____

_____

7

Systemic Yeast Infections

Yeast infections seem to be a part of daily life since the advent of antibiotics. Overuse of these drugs to treat everything from acne to hangnails has caused the unwanted effect of breeding fungus in our bodies. Women, especially, have been hard hit by these afflictions in the form of vaginal infections, and if there is yeast in the form of vaginal infection, then there is yeast everywhere else in the body!

Systemic yeast infections can be found running from the sinuses to the anus. In two cases of fibromyalgia patients who died, autopsy results found fungus growing on their brains and floating around in the cerebro spinal fluid. When the yeast is treated locally, as with vaginal infection creams, then it's bound to return. If it's treated systemically with anti-fungal medication, the cure may be worse than the disease. Talk about being between a rock and a hard place!

Anti-yeast medications, such as Nystatin, do kill off some strains of the infection, but it's a dangerous race. Which will win? The yeast dying or the liver being damaged! These medications are notoriously hepatotoxic. In many cases, what happens is the weaker strains of the fungus are killed off by the medication, and the stronger strains flourish unchecked. When the medication is withdrawn, the stronger strains seem immune to being forced out. Countering the infection with large dosages of good bacteria only helps a little.

Yeast infections have many adverse manifestations, not the least of which is the penchant of the little critters to take the carbohydrates that you eat and make alcohol out of them. That's what causes the fog in the brain of many, if not all, of the chronic yeast infection sufferers! You've got a beer factory in your gut turning out up to fourteen percent alcohol from the food you eat! Want to take a breathalyzer test? Those of you with yeast infections know that it takes a good many less drinks to get you drunk now than it used to. Is there anything that can be done to kill off the yeast? Is it possible to keep its more notable effects under control? The answer - Yes!

Are all yeast infections bad? Joe Lehmann, president of Naturally Vitamins in Phoenix, relates how a yeast colonization of the mucosal parts of the body may be a positive response to a cry for help! When the immune system is weak, he relates, yeast may build up in the body, not as an opportunistic infection, but as a defense mechanism. Yeast buds burst when they die. When they burst, they provide the body with Beta Glucan, a powerful immune enhancing nutrient. While the effects of having so much yeast living within you may be negative, there is that one bright note.

If this theory holds water, then as you convert the colonies of bad yeast to good microflora, you need to take in Beta Glucan. This will increase immune function and at the same time show the body you don't need the yeast to make Beta Glucan any more. In other words, you're telling the body that it's okay to have lowered levels of candida because its function in aiding immunity has been replaced.

I've not been an advocate of full-blown attempts to kill deeply entrenched yeast infections. Killing the patient to get to the condition is not my idea of victory against disease. There is a way of gradually whittling away at the yeast while replacing it with good microflora. At the same time, it is possible to control the production of alcohol by the yeast. The trick here is to do things slowly, allowing the therapy to get into the crooks and crannies of the body. With time (we're talking years here, so you'll have to acquire the virtue of patience), the yeast will be replaced by good bacteria. Let's take a look at my plan.

Yeast Control Program

Aerobic O-7 (Oxygen supplement)
15 - 20 drops in a full glass of water, 4 times a day
This Nascent Oxygen supplement will float around your body oxygenating your tissues. For too long we have worried about the negative effects of oxidants, forgetting that life is an oxidative process. Without oxygen you're dead! Free oxygen kills all types of germs, viruses, and funguses. This stuff not only keeps your tissues and brain well-fed with oxygen but it also helps to keep you healthy.

Molybdenum
100 mcg. - 150 mcg. Daily
This mineral acts to keep the yeast from making alcohol out of your carbohydrates.

Inulin/InuFlora
One teaspoon once or twice a day
Inulin is what's known as a probiotic. It is a sugar locked into fiber so your body can't absorb it. Inulin won't make you fat, but what it will do is provide food for the good bacteria you are trying to grow to replace the bad bacteria.

Multi strain **Acidophilus** and **Bifidus** supplement
4 capsules immediately after each teaspoon of Inulin, then 4 capsules twice more a day in-between meals.
If a liquid is used:
2 tablespoons, 3 to 4 times a day. Two of the doses should be taken <u>with</u> the Inulin. All of this needs to be taken in-between meals *and at a different time than the Aerobic O-7.*

Beta Glucan
500 mcg. Daily

Confusing? You bet. And if you're like the average chronic fatigue, fibromyalgia, or recurrent Epstein Barr patient, you are taking so many supplements and medications already that you don't know where to fit this into your schedule! It's okay, there's a lot of fudge factor involved in supplementing. It's not as demanding as taking medication.

This is food we're dealing with. You needn't be super rigid in taking in any of these supplements; make it flow as naturally as you can. Don't get highly stressed, manic, compulsive, or anal retentive about any of this. Being driven will only make any condition you have worse. Patients with chronic diseases all have lessons to learn about letting go and allowing things to happen. Sound like you?

I believe that one of the reasons we come down with chronic conditions is to force us to slow down and take a long hard look at ourselves. Examine core beliefs, throw out lists of must-haves, lose the trail of tears, and leave it all behind. If we are bright enough to figure things out, even the fifty percent mark will get us better. If you hold on to your manic-ness and think there's nothing you need to change, that this condition was heaped upon you by a capricious God, or a cruel twist of fate, then a long and debilitating illness awaits you... It's your choice.

NOTES

Timeless Voyager Press

NOTES

8

Osteoporosis
Why Doesn't All This Stuff I'm Taking Work?

I hear that line from one osteoporosis patient after another. They are taking the latest and greatest in supplements or medications. These patients are sitting around popping pills, using potions and creams with the expectation of increasing bone density. When testing time comes round, they are no better off than they were before; sometimes, the patient is even worse off. The explanation for the failure of the supplements and medicines is rather simple.

You cannot re-mineralize the bone if it doesn't want it! Your body has just spent years demineralizing the skeleton. Now you think that just because you give it all this "neat stuff" it's going to change direction and make the bones strong again. Think again! It's just like preparing a nutritious meal for an infant who doesn't want to eat. All that good chow will go sailing off the high chair and wind up on the floor. The baby doesn't have the internal demand for what you're trying to feed it!

In order to make your body demand the uptake and utilization of the supplements or medications you are eating, you must follow physiological laws. In this case, Wolfe's Law. Mineralization is laid into the bone along lines of axial stress. In other words, bones need to be compressed and pulled in order for the body to see a need to re-mineralize them. No exercise gizmo seen on TV will do it and no calisthenics, dance, or karate aerobics will accomplish the goals. ONLY one form of exercise will work to fulfill Wolfe's Law – **Progressive Resistance Exercise** – that means **using heavy weights** along with a well formulated workout.

Here is a story I believe you will find interesting. Give a horse a load of vitamins and then train that horse hard. The following day all you will see at the bottom of the stall is the usual horse poop. Give that same animal a load of vitamins and omit the training, and the next day you'll find the vitamins mostly undissolved and unabsorbed mixed in the poop. *To increase the body's absorption of nutrients, you need to create a demand. The right exercise creates that demand.*

You will need to find a real exercise expert – an exercise physiologist. This specialist should have, at the minimum, a BS degree in Exercise Science, Physical Education, or Biomechanics (Kinesiology). Most will be certified! Look for a recognized accrediting agency such as the American College of Sports Medicine, the American Society of Exercise Physiologists, the American Sports Medicine Association, or the National Strength and Conditioning Association. (There are many other associations, so do your homework. If anyone is certified in exercise and they do not have the minimum bachelor's degree in the aforementioned sciences, then they are not true experts in exercise.) These people are the REAL experts in exercise, therapeutic conditioning, and otherwise. A tight Lycra suit with a good body inside and a stack of muscle magazines in the living room does not make an expert in exercise.

When you need professional help, as with lawyers, doctors, or police, substitutes just won't do. Likewise, substitutes will not do when you are trying to increase bone density through exercise. Only guided, heavy progressive resistance exercise will work. When done properly, the increase in bone mass will be marked. Your abilities will increase as your "so-called" disabilities decrease. In my opinion, one gets weak and frail as one ages due to a lack of heavy exercise. The activities of daily living (ADL's) become harder to perform when you are lacking some form of "strenuous" exercise. Everything from lifting a skillet, blow drying your own hair, or just simply "getting up" from a chair will suffer from your lack of strength!

As you age, strength exercise is more important than cardio vascular exercise! Ninety-nine percent of what you do in a day involves strength in some way or another, not cardio vascular endurance. When was the last time you ran after the mailman because he forgot to take an important letter? Have you chased your dog for a quarter mile lately because she got loose? I doubt it!

Statistics now show that after thirty years of the aerobics craze, couch potatoes live just as long as their marathoning cousins. Longer likely, because extreme endurance exercise kills off the immune system. Distance runners and triathletes are dying off due to infection and heart disease. Yes, heart disease, the very thing they were running away from. That will be the subject for another piece. As you age, you should seek to replace disability with ability, disease with wellness. Proper weightlifting will promote both.

We should not seek to die by natural causes. The late Dr. Paul Bragg was ninety-three and surfing when he fell off the board, was knocked unconscious and drowned. After a sickly childhood, he was a healthy, stout, and vigorous man all of his adult life, never giving in to decreptitude. He did not die disabled in bed! If left to its natural progression, osteoporosis guarantees a miserable future of disability, pain and remorse. I've seen women with perfectly sharp minds lie in bed for most of the final years of their lives, scared to roll over lest they break another bone. Don't let that happen to you.

Finally, there is one more matter to be addressed. Philosophically speaking, there is another side to this diseased condition. The skeleton is the foundation and frame for the rest of the body. It carries who you are around, and gives you an external presence, a distinctive look. It shows your outer personality. What is it about the instability of your mental foundations that the outer foundation reflects? I believe that the instability, weakness, and hollowness of the frame may demand a change of mind. At the very least, a change of outlook should occur beforehand. Ponder the matter.

Program For Dealing With Osteoporosis

Nutrition and Dietary Supplements Daily

For Bones

Calcium
1600 mg.

Magnesium
1200 mg.

Boron
3 mg.

Vitamin D
500 IU

For Pain and Inflammation

Wobenzym N
3 - 5 tablets, 3 times Daily between meals

Glucosamine:
750 mg. - 1500 mg.

MSM:
500 mg. - 1000 mg.

These nutrients help lower the soft tissue irritation and joint degeneration that often accompanies osteoporosis.

EXERCISE: You must include exercise along with nutrition – **Progressive Resistance Exercise** – that means **using heavy weights** along with a well formulated workout. *To increase the body's absorption of nutrients, you need to create a demand. The right exercise creates that demand.* Bones need to be compressed and pulled in order for the body to see a need to re-mineralize them.

NOTES

_____
_____
_____
_____
_____
_____
_____
_____
_____
_____
_____
_____
_____
_____
_____
_____
_____
_____
_____
_____
_____
_____
_____

9

Longevity / Anti-Aging

For those of us who are baby boomers, who didn't want to turn 30, well, now we are all facing fifty, or worse yet, 60! Basically, we are not aging very well. All those years of sex, drugs, and rock and roll have finally taken their toll. The accumulated stress of being over-achievers, super executives, super parents, and just plain living up to YUPPIE standards have depleted our bodies. We have become susceptible to infection and degenerative disease at an earlier age than our parents. I have rehabilitated patients, boomers younger than I, who had suffered catastrophic illnesses such as strokes, massive heart attacks, and immune system failures, just to name a few.

We know now that aging is a disease process, a process of physical degeneration that begins somewhere around the twenty-seventh birthday (a fact I've repeated all too often in this book). The process begins with low enzyme levels in the body, which seriously impede the six thousand + functions that enzymes perform. We don't notice any problems at first, but as the effects multiply, we get sicker and sicker.

As you age, there is a lessening of sexual and growth hormone level production. With this drop, you lose your sexual ability, sexual drive, and your musculature. As musculature is lost, so is the ability to carry yourselves around, and daily living becomes an effort, finally ending with a depletion of the minerals that form the three tissues of the body.

This produces a breakdown of the tissues. Low zinc leads to blindness, swollen prostates, skin troubles, and slow healing. Low calcium and magnesium produce osteoporosis. Low sulfur causes connective tissue degeneration with its resultant back and joint pain. None of this need happen.

In the early days, oxidation was considered to be the cause of aging. We now know that free radical action is only a part of incurring disease. The research on enzymes and hormones makes it very clear that these are the keys to living longer, healthier, and stronger lives.

For years medicine has strived to alleviate disease and thereby brighten our lives. With its drugs and surgeries, allopathy has managed to increase life span while at the same time producing a very low quality of life. (I've worked with too many patients who were saved from death's doorway by today's "miracle medicines," only to live long painful lives. Even family and friends around them wished that they had died!) Living a longer dependant life is not the goal of longevity. Living life full of vigor and being independent are the goals to be striving towards.

While birthdays may pile up behind us, we should not accept the decrepitude that comes with aging badly. Maintaining ability, not disability, takes work. The young are not the only ones who can stave off the effects of aging. As long as there is breath, there is hope – you can put the brakes on the downhill slide at any age . It's best to start at an earlier age to preserve the most function and ability you can, but no mater where you are now, you can help yourself. Dr. Paul Bragg and Jack LaLane are sterling examples of people, once thought of as health kooks, who outlived their detractors. By combining all that is known about the process of decline and degeneration in the body, you can drive away, and even reverse, many of the effects of aging.

Soy Products

Both men and women need to stop eating soy products and their isofalvone derivatives. These soy products are estraces – analogues of estrogen. Although they are natural, they carry with them all of the potential problems of estrogen, (breast and cervical cancer in women, feminization of men and boys, etc.). Since soybeans are the largest U.S. crop, I know why the agra-business giants are pushing this stuff. But it's a mystery to me as to why health food companies are selling it. They certainly know the dangers of estrogen! There is a myth floating around that only the synthetic estraces are dangerous. I believe that most women who develop breast and uterine cancer never come in contact with the artificial stuff. It seems reasonable that their own system is out of balance, and their own estrogen is the primary culprit in the cancer! So the "natural" estraces may be as bad as the synthetic ones.

The agra-business giant, Monsanto bought out an old and well respected vitamin supplement company, Solgar, in order to get a handle on both the pharmaceutical market and the nutritional industry. They not only produce genetically modified foods but they also own Searl (the folks who brought you NutraSweet and Celebrex). Now they can use Solgar to pedal their soy by-products.

Soy is a very inferior protein, regardless of what the FDA says, and no one in the world needs any more estrogen when pesticides and environmental pollutants are full of estraces. For more information on the harm of environmental estrogen, please refer to Dr. Doris Rapp's book on allergies, Is This Your Child's World? published by Bantam.

Brain Food

Lecithin granules
2 to 3 tablespoons Daily

Your brain is sixty to seventy percent cholesterol! All of the thinking and transmitting portions of your brain are made up of cholesterol. (Next time some one calls you a fat head, thank them!)

With the anti-cholesterol diets of the last thirty years, we have sacrificed Peter to save Paul. We might have lowered our chances of heart attacks somewhat, but we have starved our brains of their essential nutrients. All MRI pictures of Alzheimer's patients show that their brains are shrunken, shriveled, and cracked. They look like molds of Jell-O left out in the open air too long. When the diet cannot provide the fat needed to maintain skin suppleness, internal inter-organ padding, and hormone manufacturing, then fat is taken from the largest available storehouse – the brain.

Over time, this constant stealing of the brain's "food" takes its toll. I'd rather die of a fast heart attack than spend ten years in bed screaming at the walls! With lecithin you get the phosphatidyl lipids needed by your brain for normal functioning. The choline and inositol in it will also lower your total cholesterol count and give you a better "good cholesterol" / "bad cholesterol" ratio. **Lecithin granules** are preferred to the capsules because it would take 12 to 19 capsules to equal one tablespoon of the granules.

Lecithin is the only soy product I recommend. I avoid recommending encapsulated products containing individualized phosphitidyl lipids because they are removed from their synergistic environment. Whole lecithin works better than any of its individual components alone. The health food industry is following the pharmaceutical industry in isolating active chemicals and offering them for sale as the latest and greatest thing. It's all hype. In all things, the synergy imposed by nature works better than the machinations imposed by man. Lecithin is cheap and works as God intended. The isolates are expensive and don't work nearly as well.

For advanced nutritional work, I suggest the teachings of Paul Bragg. Study the farsighted thinkers who recommend that one should eat different diets according to one's blood type. In many ways these teachings conflict, but it's up to you and your heart to decide which path to follow.

As always, nothing in nature is clear-cut. We cannot take one pill, eat one food, and make everything all right. The body is a multifaceted organism, and its support demands a multifaceted answer. Your car doesn't run just on gas; it takes a mixture of different fluids and electricity. If your car, which is not as complicated as your body, demands more than one thing to keep it running, then how much more will your body demand? Let's start with the basics and work our way up to the more complex issues.

Exercise

As I've stated in previous chapters, resistance exercise is a key to maintaining a strong and able body well into "old age." Find an exercise physiologist and follow their recommendations and guidance. Stay away from certified personal trainers, as most of those folks have neither the education nor the experience to treat seniors or aging boomers. "Senior strength" is not body building or beach boys showing off; it's serious life enhancing stuff much too serious to be left to amateurs.

Program For Longevity / Anti-Aging

Nutrition and Dietary Supplements Daily

Tissue Support

Epithelial (eyes, internal organs, skin)
Zinc
50 mg. - 100 mg. Daily

Connective (blood vessels and fascia)
MSM
500 mg. - 1000 mg. Daily
Osseous (bone)
Calcium
1600 mg. Daily

Magnesium
1200 mg. Daily

Timeless Voyager Press

Restoring Enzymes

Wobenzym N
5 tablets, 3 times Daily, between meals

Restoring Hormones

Progesterone Cream
1/4 teaspoon twice Daily, 12 hours apart

NOTE: Women need to read both of Dr. John Lee's books on progesterone and women's health.

Men

Androstenedione
(1) 100 mg. - 150 mg. capsule mid day between meals
(1) 100 mg. - 150 mg. capsule before bed
Or use the Androstene cream as directed

NOTE: Men, if you develop sensitivity in the nipples or pectoral area suspend taking the oral Andro. In some rare cases, men who have enough testosterone, or who convert the male hormone to the female estrogen quickly, develop gynocomasty, a feminizing condition of the breast in men. Use the andro cream with the crysin to prevent the conversion of testosterone into estrogen or into Di Hydro Testosterone.

NOTES

NOTES

10

Circulation Opening Formula/ Brain Recipe

A call came in one day from a woman very concerned about her father. Circulation studies done at Johns Hopkins found he had a ninety-five percent blockage of the arteries to his brain. As you might guess, this didn't exactly promote full brain function. This fellow was in a bad way.

The physicians there wanted to do surgery and a roto-rooter job on the arteries to open them up. The problem with that procedure is that it creates lots of little particles floating around the bloodstream that very often cause strokes. Personally, I don't know what is worse, a poorly fed, but for the most part still whole, brain, or a well-fed brain with a part of it dead? Not a good choice either way.

The woman was very distraught and wanted to know if there were any supplements that could help open the blood vessels instead of the risk of surgery. After looking through the different possibilities that can help to open up arterial occlusion, I developed the following formula:

Program For Opening Up Arterial Occlusion

Nutrition and Dietary Supplements Daily

Lecithin granules
3 tablespoons Daily

Wobenzym N
5 tablets, 4 times Daily (or 10 tablets 2 times Daily)

Vitamin E
800 IU Daily

Cayenne
(1) 200 mg. capsule, 4 times Daily
NOTE: Stomachs sensitive to the Cayenne can leave it out!

Garlic
(1) 500 mg. capsule, 2 -3 times Daily
NOTE: If the blood pressure drops down too low, leave out the garlic.

Vitamin C with bioflavonoid
1000 mg. with 500 mg. bioflavonoid twice Daily

Two months later, the same women called again to relate joyfully that the latest test found her father's carotid arteries to be 20% more open than before. Her dad was more lucid. The amazed doctors reading the results asked what had been done! Now you know, too! Whatever problems poor diets cause can be reversed by good diets.

Blood Strengthening

I may be living in a dream world of my own creation, but I would have thought that by now every doctor would know what the components of red blood cells are. I would expect them to advise their patients on how to keep their blood strong.

Apparently this simple nutritional recipe still hasn't filtered down into allopathic circles. Most physicians will tell anemic patients to take iron. What kind of iron doesn't seem important, just take it. Iron alone does not a red blood cell build.

There are three components to red corpuscles: Iron, Vitamin B 12, and Folic Acid, with the latter two in a specific balance in order to avoid throwing the B vitamin balance off. So, for the sake of those women with never-ending menstrual cycles due to thin, weak blood, for the O blood type who's mistakenly attempting to be a vegetarian, for the trauma patient who is replacing lost blood volume, and for the average Joe and Jane who fizzle out around two or three in the afternoon, here is how to build strong blood and maintain it.

Iron is the essential mineral component of blood. We need it, but not as much as we once thought. Some people hold excessive iron in their bodies and, as a result, generally do not have a problem with anemia. Iron, of the ferrous sulfate variety, kills off essential Vitamin E when both are taken together (so much for the completeness of multi vitamins).

Too much iron accruing in the colon creates a condition where the particles actually rust as they lay on the intestinal mucosa causing little ulcerations leading to inflammatory bowel diseases. Storage of too much iron has been linked to an increase in some heart conditions in men. All that having been said, iron is still essential for healthy blood.

So what kind of iron should be taken and, of course, how much? The RDA for iron is 18 mg. daily. While I've already stated elsewhere what I think of the RDA, too much iron for too long may cause problems. If blood loss has been extreme, then 50 mg. to 100 mg. daily for a week or two should be OK! After that, a daily dose of 30 mg. is safe.

Men over forty need to check the current medical advise when it comes to taking iron supplements long term. It's this group that seems to have the build-up of iron and the ensuing heart problems. Look for a chelated form of iron because it is absorbed better through the intestinal wall. Look for one that has a built in stool softener such as magnesium, to avoid the constipating effects of iron supplements. Take your Vitamin E supplements at a separate time from the iron to avoid iron's anti-E action.

Vitamin B 12 is the most neglected nutrient right now. It's gone through fads where it's been immensely popular and then been entirely forgotten. We're in the forgotten phase right now. This vitamin is the most needed component of the red blood cell. Vitamin B 12 gives the oxygen carrying punch to the cell. In order to build and maintain healthy blood, we need to take 1000 mcg. to 1200 mcg. of B 12 every day.

The oral form of this vitamin is not well absorbed because it gets destroyed by the hydrochloric acid in the stomach. What does manage to survive does not get absorbed well across the intestinal wall. Therefore, the best way to get B12 is via injection. The second best way is through sublingual absorption. A product called Sublingual B Total provides 1000 mcg. of B 12 per eyedropper at a very low cost. Of all of the B 12 supplements available, I have found people react best to this one.

Next on the list is Folic Acid. This essential nutrient is not only needed by pregnant women to insure proper spinal chord formation and protein synthesis in the fetus, it's also needed by all to avoid heart disease. The proper ratio of Folic Acid to B 12 varies somewhat according to research, but it's somewhere in the vicinity of 800 mcg. of Folic Acid to 1200 mcg. of B 12. Or, 1000 mcg. of Folic Acid to 1000 mcg. of B 12. Anywhere in that ballpark is a go.

Most people on a blood building program begin to feel better within the first week. Women don't have the energy let down during and after their cycles, athletes have greater endurance, and work-a-day folks don't feel as generally rundown as they used to.

Mental Clarity

Thinking can become a real chore in today's super high stress environments. From our early days in school to today's work and family responsibilities, we've got more to think about. More things have to be done "now" than in previous generations. Think, think, think.

We have so much on our plates, so many things to remember, so many things to do, do, do. Our minds become total chaos. Our lives have become so complicated that many of us need to carry daytimers or even mini-computers to keep the things we need to remember handy. There's simply too much stuff to keep in mind!

Our brains work on neuro-transmitters. They are not an infinite resource. As they are used and worn out, they need to be replaced. Not many doctors have ever given any thought to that fact. They became stuck on the "brain body barrier" thing, thinking that the brain was an entirely closed self-perpetuating system. Neurologists know otherwise but for some unknown reason the information doesn't trickle down. In these politically correct days, the anti-heart disease diets have depleted our brains of the "foods" we need to think. What's one got to do with the other? Confused? Let me explain.

As I said before, the human brain is sixty to seventy percent cholesterol. Yes, your brain is made up of all that nasty stuff your doctor has told you to stay away from for the sake of your heart. The problem is that until recently (the last ten years or so), your doctor probably did not know the difference between the good cholesterol and the bad cholesterol. Within the last decade, allopathic medicine has caught up with Naturopathic in its recognition that some cholesterol is needed for life and health. Too late for some, I might add.

Let's get back to neuro-transmitters. All the thinking parts of your brain, the neurotransmitters, are made of cholesterol. With the nonspecific ban on the eating of cholesterol, many have depleted their brains of the material needed to renew their stock of neurotransmitters.

The body needs a steady stream of good cholesterol. Without fats, you would be dead. Cholesterol is used to make hormones. Hormones, especially the sexual hormones, are the fountains of youth. These can only be made of high quality cholesterol and usually the vegetable variety just does not cut it. Look around at most committed vegetarians. If they have been at it for more than a decade, I guarantee you that they look 10 to 15 years older than their chronological age. There is a reason for that – lowered sexual hormone production. Animal cholesterol is the body's preferred choice for whittling down into a hormone. With some exceptions, notably Mexican yam, no vegetable source will really make testosterone or progesterone.

We need cholesterol to make internal organ padding. We don't think much about the way our bodies protect the viscera inside of us, but it does so with brown fat. Without these bundles and layers of fat, the internal organs would rub against each other and bruise. They would be traumatized by the little bumps and knocks of life. Silly you say? No, we've examples of just such trauma in bodybuilders and endurance athletes. They strive for extremely low body fat levels. In many who have attained body fat levels under 6%, internal injuries are common.

We need cholesterol for skin suppleness. Without the oils, maintaining soft supple skin would be all but impossible. We would feel and move like old dried up cowhide. Notice how people with more oily skin have fewer wrinkles over time. Notice how skinnier seniors have more fallen faces and show the signs of age in their hands and skin more than their stouter compatriots. Cholesterol makes the difference.

Most importantly, you need cholesterol for brain transmission. It all depends on fat. Look at the MRI pictures of Alzheimer's patients' brains. Their brains look like Jell-O that has been left out on a table for week! Shrunken, dried, and cracked! I'll bet you dollars to doughnuts they ardently listened to their doctors' advice about keeping dietary cholesterol down! There are no fat people in Alzheimer's wards!

You can protect your heart against bad cholesterol and feed your brain all of the good stuff it needs to keep it functioning at high levels for life! And you can get most of the brain nutrients you need from one inexpensive source – Lecithin.

The most important neuro transmitters are the phosphatidyl lipids (fats) choline, inositol, and serine. Today they are available, separated from their natural environment in many brain-boosting products.

The problem with the separation aspect is this. Nature made these nutrients to work in conjunction with each other, not separately in their synergistic (helper) environments. We don't know how well they work when separated from all of the things nature wrapped around them to help them work. When any company, whether a drug or a vitamin firm, separates a nutrient from its synergistic environment and markets it separately, or compounds it with some other things, they usually boost the price sky high.

For example, there are 1700 mg. of Choline in the average tablespoon of lecithin. Lecithin costs four dollars a pound. Isolated Choline and Serine supplements contain sixty to one hundred capsules of 300 mgs. and sells for over twenty dollars a bottle. You're getting much less nutrient for a lot more money. There is no assurance that it will work right once it's been isolated from the rest of the natural nutrients.

The nerves need B Complex vitamins to work right. Without sufficient B, nerves don't fire off and the messages don't get received. So we need to add them as well. Finally, everything works better when fish oils are added to the mix of fats provided to the brain. Add vitamin E and Coenzyme Q-10 for their antioxidant and neuro-protective effects, and you have the Brain Recipe.

The Brain Recipe

Nutrition and Dietary Supplements Daily

Lecithin granules
1 tablespoon Daily
Sprinkle it on food, mix it with drinks, or just plain pop a spoonful in your mouth and wash it down with a few swigs of water (don't' chew before swallowing, just hold the granules then swallow).

B – Complex
(1) Balanced B – 50 or B – 100 Daily

Fish Oils
(1) tablespoon Daily (Any way you can get the stuff down)

Vitamin E
400 IU - 800 IU Daily

Co Enzyme Q-10
30 mg. - 50 mg. Daily

Not only will following this program improve brain function in the long and short term, it's also dandy for lowering the bad cholesterol in the body. To prove it to yourself, have a blood cholesterol count done, follow the program for a month, and then have another test done. You'll be a believer!

NOTES

Timeless Voyager Press

NOTES

_____
_____
_____
_____
_____
_____
_____
_____
_____
_____
_____
_____
_____
_____
_____
_____
_____
_____
_____
_____
_____
_____
_____
_____
_____
_____
_____
_____
_____
_____

Epilogue

We have looked briefly into each of the subjects I've covered and have dealt mainly with the remedies for each. I've tried not to bore you with needless facts and figures, commonly used as fillers in books of this type, about the number of people who have these ailments. If you are suffering, you want to get to the meat of the subject, not linger torturously in the fluff authors write because their subject doesn't have enough depth to fill an article, much less a book.

The ability to present ideas concisely is both a blessing and a curse. It's a blessing in the sense that thoughts and concepts can be communicated with great depth and understanding using as few words as possible. Lincoln's Gettysburg address is a wonderful example of that. Presenting ideas concisely becomes a curse when it's time to write a thesis (I've written two). Most boards appear to care more about the quantity of your communication than the quality.

One professor I studied with said that his doctoral board chairman took his thesis, unclasped it, and tossed the work down a flight of stairs.

" If it makes it to the next landing, you've got your degree," he said.

It didn't. So his wife, a screenwriter with, as the professor described it, the "ability to vomit words onto paper," rewrote his work. She literally doubled its size and it immediately passed muster. The next time, not only did it make it to the next landing, the tome went down the next flight of stairs as well!

In real life, I'm fairly verbose. My wife says I become professorial or preachy. Very true, but unlike most of my colleagues, who have little to say in the treatment room and much to laud themselves for on paper, I'm the opposite. I like to sit and chat with patients awhile, taking the time to cover their concerns and questions. You can't fit in umpteen numbers of folks in a day that way, but you can look at yourself in the mirror knowing you haven't short-changed anyone. Though I must admit it doesn't always make for success in paying the overhead.

Most of the areas covered in this book are fairly complex. Mountains of material could likely have been heaped onto each chapter. But I settled for a brief introduction to the problem with some of the history of the condition when applicable. I've included the remedies and any other teachings that I believe needed to be covered. Over the years, I've found that any patient with a chronic condition knows more about their plight and its causes / effects than I do. What I've presented here, brief as it may be, is a different understanding of these conditions along with a simplified explanation of their likely effects.

To those who truly seek healing, take this information and run with it. Take charge of your own life and healing, get well, and carry on. Take your life to a higher level of well being with all of the blessings and joy that it brings.

To those who are waiting for someone else to come, do some magic, and heal you, or to invent some wonder drug to cure you, in my opinion, you'll never get better. In medical jargon, you are achieving secondary gain. You're getting attention from being sick, punishing yourself for something, or using your sickness as an excuse not to function in society while manipulating those around you.

I truly feel sorry if you're wasting your existence and making those around you miserable. In so doing, you are affecting more lives, adversely, than you know. Ultimately, you are the final arbiters of your own fate. God made this the universe of free choice. With whatever path you choose there are consequences, good and bad, for that path. The path of enlightenment and well being has more good lessons than bad ones. This path will bring you to more inner peace, love, and light than any other.

I wish for all of you to find the spark of the Creator that lives within you. Nourish that spark so that it grows into a flame, uniting you in spirit with the ultimate force for healing and for good. Be well, and God bless you all.